LEARNING CENTRES

I would like to dedicate this book to June Eileen Scott, without whose support and belief it would have not come to fruition, and to Peter Bennett for giving me the opportunity to write it.

LEARNING CENTRES

A Step-by-step Guide to Planning, Managing and Evaluating
an Organizational Resource Centre

Amanda Scott

**KOGAN
PAGE**

London ● Stirling (USA)

First published in 1997

Kogan Page Limited
120 Pentonville Road
London N1 9JN
and
22883 Quicksilver Drive
Stirling, VA 20166, USA

British Library Cataloguing in Publication Data

A CIP record for this book is available from the British Library.

ISBN 0 7494 2293 9

Typeset by JS Typesetting, Wellingborough, Northants.
Printed and bound in Great Britain by Biddles Ltd, Guildford and King's Lynn.

Contents

Foreword   xi

Acknowledgements   xv

1. Introduction   1

The move towards resource-based learning   1

What is an open learning centre?   2

Self-development – a natural process?   3

2. Identifying the Need   7

Preparing the way for change   9

Dealing with resistance: Preparing for battle   10

Overcoming resistance: Self-development workshops   11

3. Selling the Idea   13

Getting support from the top   13

Current business initiatives: The trial-sized package and
    the 'freebie'   14

The transition from baby food to solids   15

4. How Long Will It Take and How Much Is It Going to Cost? 19
Recommended timescales 19
The cost 20
Other forms of financial support 21

5. Starting the Project 23
The first step 23
Working parties 23
Size – is bigger better? 25
Opening hours: Burning the midnight oil 27
Security 28
Damaged goods 29
Marketing internally: Finding out what they want 29
Learning styles 30
Competition time 30
Making a corporate video 31

6. Resourcing the Centre 33
The product mix: How do you decide what to put in it? 33
Selecting the media 34
Assessing suitability 36
Evaluating the resources 37
Resources fair 38
What will your user use? 39
How do you know what will work? 39

7. Types of Resource: What's Available and What Will it Cost? 41
Workbooks 41
Audio 42
Video 43
Books: Identifying the bookworms 45

8. Multimedia **51**
CD-I versus CD-ROM 54
The benefits of CD-I 55
The future of CD-I 56
Revolving libraries 56
Computer-based training (CBT) 58
Self-diagnostics 59

9. Non-vocational Materials **61**
Is there a need? 61
Parlez-vous Français? 62
Career development 64
The Internet: Does it have a place in the learning centre? 64
Cybercafé 65
The dangers 66
Alternative media: Games and activities 66
Health and safety 68
Professional qualifications 69
Journals and periodicals 69
Resources to develop study skills 70
Senior management resources 70

10. Logistics **73**
Cataloguing the material 73

11. The Launch **75**
Promotional materials 78
Feedback: What did they think? 81
Launch programme ideas 82

12. Administration and Logistics **83**
Evaluation methods 83
The manager's role in the evaluation process 86
Information systems 87

Contents

The learning centre catalogue 87
Service questionnaires 89
Management of the centre 90
The best person for the job 91
The role of the administrator 92
When demand exceeds supply 93
Complementing the training courses 97
The learning environment 97
Making the most of your cupboard 100
Support 102
Setting up multiple sites 104
International open learning centres 107
Marketing your centre 108
The relaunch 109
Women 111
Older employees 113
Younger employees 113
The family 115
Meetings 116
Technology days 116
Induction 117
Language learning 118
Revision facilities 119
Roadshows 120
The learning bus 123
Newsletters 124
New products 126
Breakfast launches 126
The learning club – membership, social events etc 127
Learning incentives 131
Learning sets 132
The future of the learning centre 133

13. Case Studies **135**
Royal Marsden NHS Trust 135
London Ambulance Service 142
Virgin Atlantic Airways 149
Victoria and Albert Museum 154
Heathrow Airport Ltd 159
SIMS Education Services Ltd 165

Appendices
I   Forms and questionnaires 169
II   Recommended reading 177
III Sample catalogue formats 185
IV   Sample screens from Resource Manager, OLC
     Management, Administration and Reporting
     System 191
V   Sample OLC Launch Poster 201
VI   Resource Manager 205

Index 211

Foreword

It is a widely held view that learning centres offer an excellent solution to the learning and training needs of organizations. In theory, that is exactly what they should do. In practice, most of them just don't work – and that is exactly why this book was written.

What are the objectives of this book?

Quite simply, the objectives of the book are to ensure that the final statement above eventually becomes confined to fiction rather than reality.

This is, of course, dependent on organizations taking training and learning seriously, and it is a matter of some conjecture as to whether most of them do. Lip-service is a cliché in the training fraternity, but how many organizations do you know that subsequently continue to live up to their Investors in People Award, once it has been achieved?

The book aims to dispel some of the myths about learning centres and attempts to illustrate best practice through case studies and through experience gained over several years by observation and involvement.

The book aims to introduce you to new thoughts, ideas and suggestions, it is not a simple regurgitation of existing bland approaches, or facts and figures. Amanda Scott, along with all of us at Learning Resources International, is a firm believer that tradition has no place where learning is concerned, and that almost any route is acceptable if it achieves a successful outcome, from the point of view of changing organizational attitudes and individual skills.

The book is designed to be both a working and a reference tool, a source of ideas and advice that will constantly be on hand, as well as a source of inspiration.

Who is the book aimed at?

When we were discussing the focus of the book in its early days, it was decided that it would be written in a way that would appeal to several audiences, and that it would offer practical advice, fresh ideas and convincing arguments and evidence that learning centres are and should be a permanent element in the matrix of training and learning for any organization. So the audience is deliberately mixed, as follows.

Training and development strategists and implementers

Those responsible for policy and strategy within an organization, enabling them to have an insight into how learning centres should form an integral part of the training matrix.

Learning resource centre/open learning centre administrators and managers

Those responsible for the day-to-day running of the centres. Those responsible for supervising the learning and the processes around it, and those who provide the expertise and advice so necessary for the success of any centre.

Directors and budget holders

Invariably initiatives have to be financed and funded. This book is designed to enlighten those responsible for sanctioning budget approval as to the value of the investment for the growth of the organization, and all the implications and considerations for these initiatives to be successful.

Operational managers

Possibly the most critical link in the success chain of learning centre initiatives, operational managers can either support or distance themselves and thus stifle the success of such initiatives. This book is designed to highlight their responsibilities and to illustrate the benefits to themselves, their teams and to the bottom line, of supporting such moves wholeheartedly.

Peter Bennett, Learning Resources International

Acknowledgements

I would like to thank the following organizations for allowing me to feature their learning centres in this book: Lorraine Stanley of the Royal Marsden NHS Trust, Tom Martin Herbert of the London Ambulance Service, Bob Creedy of SIMS Education Services Ltd, John Prior of Heathrow Airport Ltd, Katherine Cornish of the Victoria and Albert Museum, and David Innes of Virgin Atlantic Airways.

I would also like to thank Philip Mudd and his team at Kogan Page for their invaluable assistance; Rachel Broome, training consultant, for tying up the 'loose ends' and, last but not least, all my friends and colleagues at Learning Resources International Ltd for their continued support.

Amanda Scott

Chapter 1

Introduction

The move towards resource-based learning

Over the last few years there has been a significant change in the field of training and development. One of these changes has been the move away from more traditional styles of training to resource-based development. Why has this change occurred? It could be for several reasons – to cut costs, to increase individuals' self-worth and/or reduce levels of absenteeism. Whatever the reason for this change in the training culture, we can be certain of one thing: these changes are going to continue, with evidence suggesting that resource-based learning is a significant move and one that is here to stay.

As with all change no one can ever be certain how long it will last, and indeed how long it will be before we go back to the more traditional routes, as primary school teaching staff are beginning to find.

If we are to accept that resource-based learning is a route that our organizations want to take, we need to fully understand what it means. This book has been written to provide you with some guidance and support, to assist you and your organization when passing through this transition. As the title suggests, the key area within self-development has been the setting up of a corporate learning centre. The objective of this book is therefore to provide you with a step-by-step guide to setting up a learning centre and to provide advice on how it can be maintained and marketed successfully. But before we move on to the first area, I would like to discuss is what is actually meant by a 'learning centre'.

What is an open learning centre?

There has been an enormous amount of confusion over the past few years as to what an open learning centre actually is. I decided to ask a few people within training and development to answer this question. Here are a few of their replies.

> 'It is a place where people can go to acquire new skills or improve on existing ones.'
> 'A library of resources, mostly text based, that allow people to develop in areas that may not be covered by training courses.'
> 'Anything from a multimedia station to an audio player.'
> 'It's a bit like a library, isn't it?'

As you can see, the responses are varied and do not give as clear a definition as we might have hoped. Perhaps this is because there is no such thing as a model open learning centre; a learning centre is a mechanism, it is a path that people can take, and there is no right or wrong way of doing it. There are, however, standard elements that every successful learning centre will contain and these will be discussed within the various sections of this book.

tohere

Self-development – a natural process?

Why have we moved towards resource-based learning? Many organizations feel that individual employees are better able to develop and grow if they are pushed into taking more responsibility for their own development. Why should the training department be responsible for everything? Shouldn't it exist to provide support and assistance rather than spoon-feeding individuals?

From an early age we are not given the opportunity to take responsibility for our own learning, we are pushed into it. At primary school our objective is to learn to read and write and to develop some of the basic social skills, our area of self-development at this age is very limited. We then move on to secondary school where we attend classes and are fed information, which we are then obliged to digest and regurgitate at the end of each year in the form of an exam. It is therefore not in our natures to demand information, just as it is not a natural desire to develop ourselves, and this is largely because it has always been done for us.

Can you remember a situation at school where you did not understand something and asked if there was another way in which you could acquire this knowledge? The situation does not change dramatically even when we move on to higher education, where from day one we are given recommended book lists. Our choices have already been limited, and if reading does not tie in with our preferred method of learning, tough. If we have gone through a third of our lives in this manner, changing is not going to be an easy task; it is not natural for us to suddenly want to read a book or watch a video, we would much rather go on a course because this is what we have always done. And the attitude of managers has been to pass their staff problems through to the training department, who will solve an immediate difficulty by placing the individual on a course.

I am not by any means suggesting that there is no value in attending a training course, and I do not believe that traditional, classroom-based training will ever be completely replaced. People will always benefit from the interaction they gain from participating in the dynamics of a course, and courses also give employees the chance to get away from their working environment – but I do not need to sell the benefits of training to you. It has, however, been recognized that a course is not always the best option or the most effective one for some employees.

The whole transition towards resource-based learning is a positive step to encouraging individual development, which is perhaps the result of the increased move towards the creation of a more empowered workforce. Sceptics would say that 'empowerment' is another word for cost-cutting, but I believe that it is a valuable process through which we are creating an 'enabling' environment, one where employees are able to take full responsibility for their careers, their work, their staff, the development of their staff and their own development.

We have all come to accept that the days of a job for life and the 9 to 5 routine are long gone; people are giving more to their organizations and as a consequence want more from their jobs. After all, we spend the majority of our daily lives in the workplace, and if we do not feel that we are personally benefiting ourselves and others, we may begin to put less in, and as a consequence get very little out. By allowing individuals to take responsibility for their development needs, the result could be an increase in motivation, self-worth, more individuals taking ownership of their role and a significant increase in awareness of their employees' needs.

You may feel that it is asking too much of an already overworked individual to take on additional responsibility, ie that of self-development. What I am suggesting is that organizations identify their own needs and those of their staff, and when they have identified those needs they will be required to develop them. This demand is huge when you consider that all managers had to do in the past was pick up a telephone and call the training department. If staff can identify their own needs, surely it is more likely that they will want to do something about them, and will be motivated to do so. There will be a battle, as I said, because self-development is not natural. So the next question is what do we do to help them through the transition? One of the answers may be to set up a learning centre.

Chapter 2

Identifying the Need

How do you decide that an open learning centre is the right solution for you? Many organizations embark on such a move for very different reasons. One reason may be that their competitors have all got one (the 'keeping up with the Joneses' attitude), while others have done so because the organization really believes that there should be a transition towards self-development. Whatever the reason, ie cost, increase in staff motivation etc, you need to look at whether you really need the centre. Setting one up is not inexpensive and it can be a huge write-off if not handled correctly, affecting not only your credibility but the credibility of the training and HR functions.

Many organizations that have set up learning centres, and according to recent figures within an Industrial Society report this includes over 40 per cent, have done so at great expense because they imposed it upon their employees; they have not stopped to ask themselves whether it is something they really need. The senior managers and the training department might, but all too few organizations really carry out a thorough needs analysis. Part of making the centre successful is ensuring that you have a market for it in the first place. Consider marketing departments, which do not go to all the effort of creating a new product until they are certain that there are people who will want what they are going to develop. The point is that you must do your market research first – do you have a potential customer? If you do, find out what they really want and need.

You may feel that this is totally unnecessary, because not everyone is going to admit to having a training need. But learning centres do not suit everyone's organization. You may be in the situation where people are getting the most they can from the courses that you run; you may have employees who have undergone so much change recently that this will be the final straw and you will lose all credibility by trying to introduce yet another change.

Of course, there are organizations for which a learning centre is not the right solution, and you need to make sure that you are not one of them. It may also be that you simply do not have the time or resources to set up a learning centre, you may not have the space, the senior management may have other ideas; it is up to you to distinguish between these, and make a decision on the route that you wish to take. And just because you cannot have a learning centre does not meant that you cannot create an environment of which resource-based learning and self-development is a part. There are many organizations that have decided not to take the route of the open learning centre, but that have nonetheless successfully succeeded in dramatically changing the learning culture within their organizations. Some have created an environment where individuals are responsible for their own development but do not turn to a learning centre for the solution – instead they have provided the individual with a range of alternatives, from work-based activities to their own budget from which they can purchase their own resources.

How do you find out if a learning centre is the right solution for you? First of all you need to be sure that employees would be prepared to use it. Do they want to take responsibility for their own learning? Before you decide that a learning centre is the perfect answer it is worth considering the following.

Checklist

☐ What are the benefits of an open learning centre to your organization?
☐ Do you have adequate space or can it be created?
☐ Do you have commitment from the senior managers?
☐ Do you have any resistance from the training department?
☐ What do the managers think?
☐ How will you obtain a suitable budget?

Only after you have found out this information, through whatever means, can you begin the next phase.

Preparing the way for change

Once you have decided that the learning centre is the right solution for your needs you then need to start preparing the organization for the change in the role of training and development – prepare it for self-development. This is not an easy task, and involves a lot of patience, energy and commitment from all parties. Although self-development is not a natural process for most people, there will of course be some who want to absorb learning and who relish the thought of a learning centre where they will find all the solutions to their needs. But what about

9

the majority of those within the organization who are not so keen? How are you going to get them to change the habits that they have adopted, and become accustomed to, over the past 20 years?

Many organizations feel that this change in culture can take place in a matter of months, even weeks. It would be great if this were true, but unfortunately it is not, and the move away from the comfort blanket of the training department is not an easy one. Never forget what you are asking of people. You are in fact saying 'We are opening a learning centre, we are spending a lot of money on it and we want you to use all the facilities that we are providing as often as you can, and we would like you to do this in your own time!' If it is put across in this manner, do you really think they will be queuing at the door when you open?

> Always bear in mind that people will be thinking that the learning centre is being set up because the training department cannot be bothered to run courses any more, or that the organization simply wants to cut costs.

Dealing with resistance: Preparing for battle

Expect a huge amount of resistance from employees. You may be excited about the whole project and see nothing but huge advantages, but never forget to put yourself in your customers' shoes. Prepare yourself for opposition – if you anticipate some difficulties then you will be saving yourself a lot of potential future problems. Make a checklist of all the potential obstructions to the project, and write down how you will overcome each of these. Some of the arguments you may hear are as follows.

'I won't have the time.'
'I don't have the patience.'
'It's too far to go.'
'There won't be anything there for me.'
'I'm not motivated enough.'
'My manager will not release me.'
'I have a family to look after.'
'I spend enough time at work.'
'I do not want to spend my own time there.'

Activity

List a few other objections that you anticipate receiving.

Overcoming resistance: Self-development workshops

One idea, which has worked in many organizations, is the implementation of self-development workshops. These workshops can be held to provide key staff with an awareness of self-development as well as providing you with a mechanism through which to sell the learning centre. These workshops can contain various elements, but the overall objective should be to increase awareness and general understanding of the development process. It might also include helping staff to develop others, with an insight into how people learn, how to identify development needs, how resource-based learning can be used as a solution to these needs, and how the learning centre can provide some of the solutions.

Some organizations that have implemented these workshops have then gone one step further, by identifying 'development champions'. These are people within the organization who have demonstrated a large degree of enthusiasm and commitment to self-development. These champions can be very useful when selling the learning centre concept, especially to others who are a little more sceptical. The more people you can get excited about the project the better, especially during the initial stages, it could make your job a lot easier.

Chapter 3

Selling the Idea

Getting support from the top

Never underestimate the power of influence. The more senior managers you get involved in the process the better, although this is not always possible. Even when it is possible it is rarely easy to convince senior managers that they need to donate some of their valuable time to help you.

If you can get them on board and recruit one or two as champions then gaining other people's commitment will be that much easier. Put yourself in the place of a pyramid salesperson – get one person excited in the project, give them the opportunity to sell to others and let the process continue, and within six months you could have the majority of the organization selling the benefits.

Of course, it is easy to say all this and quite another thing to do it. Like anything else it takes time and energy. You may find that at the beginning you have plenty of energy but have not been allocated very much time.

All too often it is the case that the team responsible for setting up the project is not given adequate time to implement it effectively. The board are reluctant for you to spend too much time on the project, let alone free others to help you – how difficult can it be? All you need to do is buy a few machines and some books! If this is the reaction that you anticipate receiving you must set down guidelines from the start, and ensure that the board know exactly what is involved. Not only do you need to sell the concept, you need to make certain that they are aware of the potential resistance that may occur.

 **Key point**

State exactly what you will need to make it work. If the learning centre fails, initially it will be a reflection on you, but it will ultimately be a reflection of the organization for which you work.

Current business initiatives: The trial-sized package and the 'freebie'

There are other ways in which you can prepare the organization for this learning shift. Think about initiatives that the organization is going through currently, or is likely to in the near future; make the tools available wherever and whenever you can. Employ the tactics of advertising agencies or salespeople, tempt people with what will be available to them in the near future, get them thinking immediately about how they can use resource-based learning in a whole range of situations. For example, think of how our buying patterns are made to change when a new product is launched, there are advertisements, but there are also trial-sized packs available – how often do you receive freebies in a magazine, at the supermarket, on the street and in the post?

Millions of pounds are spent by organizations every year on these marketing ploys. How does this link to the learning centre scenario? Well, why do we receive freebies? People want us to try their product, they want us to move away from our usual product to a new one, and the only way we would change from using our existing product would be if we tried something new and it was significantly better or cheaper, but without trying it first we would not know if it was better. We may change as a result of a personal recommendation, but we certainly are not going to go out and buy it – we may not like it. If it was free, this would be a completely different ball game. Why not try this with self-development – let people try it, entice them, but find situations when you know they would most use it. Are you more likely to accept a free chocolate bar at lunchtime or first thing in the morning?

The transition from baby food to solids

Offering tasters is one idea but you could also think of other ways in which you can get people to use resource-based material. It is a good idea to instigate change over a period of time as it should be a gradual process rather than a complete transition from formal training to self-development. The best way to change people's dependencies is by using a gradual approach – the best diets are those which involve a complete change in attitude to eating habits; we are all too familiar with the ineffectiveness of 'crash dieting' and the yo-yo effect this has. If you really want to change people's habits the best way to do this and achieve a long-term effect is via a staged approach, and there are several techniques for this.

🗝 Key point

If you know that the organization is going to be using a new software package, encourage people to use other solutions to help them understand the packages. Why not make a set of resources available to each department? This may include books, computer-based (CBT) training packages or a video which covers these applications. If the organization does not have the resource to do this for each department then make just a few sets that can be loaned out. Get the support of the information technology department, ask them to recommend titles to individuals on each of their courses.

🗝 Key point

You can also do this with skills training courses. Suggest a recommended reading list for each of the courses, which could be handed out either in advance or after the course.

🗝 Key point

If the senior managers remain unconvinced, organize for someone who has a learning centre to come and talk to them or, better still, arrange a visit to see a learning centre in operation. Do not worry about approaching other organizations – most are more than happy to show off their pride and joy, especially if the project has proved successful, and it will help to dispel any misconceptions that the senior managers may have. It will also give them an indication of the work that is involved in setting up a learning centre and will help you gain their support.

- Hold self-development workshops.
- Nominate development champions.
- Offer 'freebies'.
- Link resource-based learning to IT development initiatives.
- Organize visits/talks for senior managers.

Once you have begun to change the way people think about their own development you can start to set up the centre, but do not forget that you have to continue with the sales process. All too often people get so wrapped up in the process of setting up the centre that they forget about the continual process of change that is taking place for everyone around them.

Ensure that the managers are informed of the stage you are at and involve them as much as is possible in the process. If you forget them they will quickly lose interest and they will not assist you in the selling process once the centre is up and running.

Summary

- Prepare yourself for resistance.
- Make a checklist of all the possible objections to the project.
- Think about how you will overcome these.
- Implement self-development workshops.
- Nominate development champions.
- Think about current and future initiatives.
- Suggest alternative solutions for software training.
- Offer reading lists that complement the current training courses.
- Invite a speaker to give a discussion on the benefits of open learning centres.
- Involve as many people as you can in the setting up process of the centre.

Chapter 4

How Long Will It Take and How Much Is It Going to Cost?

Recommended timescales

It is very difficult to put an exact time limit on setting up a learning centre, as it is dependent on so many factors, including of course the culture of your own particular organization. On average most learning centres take anything from 6 to 18 months to set up – this usually means from submission of the project to launch. But do not be too hard on yourself if you cannot complete within this timescale; try not to impose too many limitations as you will only end up feeling disheartened and demotivated if the project is delayed. I am not suggesting that you should not have a deadline or goal set in place, but allow some flexibility. It may be that the room you have earmarked for the centre is no longer available, your budget may be needed elsewhere, it may take longer than you had anticipated to gain approval. You should set yourself mini-targets that can be achieved over a longer period of time. For example, in two months you will have gained approval, by month four you will have a room, etc. If you do it this way you will not feel that your time has been totally wasted if the project has to be put on hold for any reason.

The cost

How much is it going to cost and how can you justify it to your organization?

It is not easy to put a price on the value of learning and even less easy to say that setting up a learning centre is going to cost £X. Most of the centres that Learning Resources International Ltd have helped set up have had a budget of anywhere between twenty and forty thousand pounds. This is the budget that is often allocated to the acquisition of resources and excludes the cost of hardware and of course marketing, furnishing the actual centre, etc. I have included sample costs that other organizations have met when setting up centres but remember that each centre is unique – and as such your needs may be very different, and this will of course affect the budget that you request. If you cannot obtain this amount of budget, you should not feel excluded from setting up a resource centre. Some centres have had budgets as low as £2,000 to work with and I have included a chapter on how you can set up a resource centre with such a limited amount of resource.

Here is a list of potential costs that you may need to budget for.

- hardware
- resources
- environment/furniture
- promotional material
- use of consultants
- marketing
- the launch
- catalogue production
- staff costs
- administrative systems
- future resources
- support.

Once you have analysed the costs involved in setting up an open learning centre you need to prepare yourself for battle. Make sure that you are well prepared before you put the proposal to the board. It may be that they have already outlined a budget for the centre; if they have not then make sure that you have plenty of benefits to throw at them.

! Tip

If you time it well you could get some free hardware on purchasing CD-ROM courses – keep your eye out for the special offers.

Other forms of financial support

These include government funding, the Training and Enterprise Councils (TECs), Investors in People.

Chapter 5

Starting the Project

The first step

Now you have two projects on board, you are selling the concept of self-development and starting to set up your learning centre. You have a lot to do and, more than likely, not a lot of time to do it in. Seek help. Why take it all on yourself? The more the merrier.

Working parties

Many organizations set up working parties to distribute the tasks involved among a number of highly capable individuals. A working party can be the perfect solution – but how do you decide who should be a part of it? For example, should you invite people who are external to the training department? Should you ask senior managers? In our experience some of the most successful working parties or project teams have included a mix of people, with a good combination of abilities from a range of backgrounds. There are many advantages and few disadvantages to doing this. Inviting people from all levels within the organization will help you in the selling process, reducing the threat of potential resistance. It will also help you understand the requirements of a wider range of individuals and therefore enable you make a better choice when it comes to the media mix.

A mixed group acts as a great catalyst for developing enthusiasm in self-development. Many working parties have included front-line staff, trainers, IT people and line managers. The advantages of having an IT person are enormous, as if you are going to have multimedia stations it is always of benefit to have someone on board who knows what they are talking about. The last thing you want is to end up being sold to by some salesperson, which results in you acquiring all the wrong resources for the specification of computer that you have.

Once you have decided upon your working party you may want to elect a project leader, although this is not always necessary – a collective approach may prove as effective.

Ensure that meetings are held regularly and that everyone in the team is really committed to the project. The last thing you want is for people to start not turning up and letting you down due to other work commitments, as this will only leave you feeling demoralized and demotivated.

☞ Key point

It is also a good idea to hold meetings away from the working environment, somewhere where you cannot be contacted. This will give you the opportunity to have good, quality time to sit and discuss the next stage of the project.

You may want to allocate particular tasks to individuals. If you do have someone who is responsible for IT, give them the responsibility of the multimedia etc. Delegate according to skills, wherever possible having someone who has a creative mind– someone from the marketing or sales department is always a bonus as they can provide you with good ideas on how to market and sell the concept. It is also a good idea to give an individual responsibility for the actual physical appearance of the room as this can be a time-consuming activity. Pool your resources, make the most of the skills and resources that are available to you, but make sure that at the end of each meeting minutes are typed and action lists made. This will help you stick to deadlines and ensure that everyone in the team is doing what they should when they should.

Checklist

☐ Select members of the team.
☐ Identify key skills.
☐ Get commitment.
☐ Lay groundrules.
☐ Set timescales.
☐ Allocate tasks.
☐ Meet regularly.
☐ Agree next course of action.
☐ Review progress.

Size – is bigger better?

Just how big should your learning centre be? There really is no statutory requirement or indeed any evidence that suggests that a large learning centre is likely to be more effective than a smaller one; it really depends on your own particular organization and culture. If, for example, you only have 100 employees who will have access to the centre, a huge centre is not going to be necessary. Size is also dependent on the room that you have available to you – in reality you probably will not have a choice of locations for your learning centre and will have to make the most of what you are given. This is one of the main hurdles that organizations encounter when setting up a resource centre; many are delayed due to internal politics and fights over room availability.

Of course, there are organizations that are extremely fortunate and have a choice of location, but the majority do not. Do not despair if the room that you are finally allocated is not quite as large as you had hoped for, there are distinct advantages to having a small centre, for example at least it will always look busy and well stocked. There is to my mind nothing worse than seeing a huge centre, beautifully kitted out, which is completely empty. Many organizations that do suffer from learning cupboards soon prove their worth and are allocated more space as time goes by, whereas those that are overrun with space and have an empty centre are looked upon with resentment from those staff who were bidding for that particular site.

The disadvantages of a small centre are that you may soon find yourself turning people away from the centre due to lack of space, which will obviously affect the credibility of the centre and its value. It is not easy to find a happy medium, but perhaps if you do have limited space then you should market the centre as more of a distribution centre/distance library, or make it available to a smaller sector of people initially with a view to expanding as soon as you have adequate space.

Opening hours: Burning the midnight oil

This is a bone of contention for many organizations. It would be great to have the centre open 24 hours a day, 7 days a week, but you really need to consider whether this is logistically possible, and whether it is necessary. This is where your market research will prove invaluable. When you send out your initial questionnaire why not ask when people are most likely to use the centre. You then monitor the usage of the centre during the first three months and if you find that no one is using it at seven o'clock in the evening, you have two options: either try marketing that time by organizing specific events etc, or close the centre earlier.

The other issue is one which is perhaps even more politically explosive – when will people be given the opportunity to use the centre? Will people be allowed time to use it during work time or will use be restricted to lunch hours and after work? I strongly believe that people should be given the time to use the centre during the working day. There are distinct advantages to this, because if people are expected to go in their own time they are less likely to make use of it and may feel that the organization is not investing in them at all but merely trying to cut costs; this will result in a feeling of resentment and you may have a very empty open learning centre as a consequence.

Commitment from senior managers is essential, but I do appreciate that it is difficult. Many organizations are having to rationalize quite dramatically, people are working long hours in the fear that they may lose their jobs if they don't, and the last thing managers want to do is to start releasing people to go to the learning centre, especially if they feel that they are only going there to brush up their language skills! It is strongly advised that a strategy for supporting learning through 'permitted development time' is put in place and agreed beforehand at the highest possible level. Make sure that the managers are aware of their part in the process.

It may be that individuals are given a certain amount of time they are allowed to use the centre per week or per month. You may even want to supply individuals with vouchers of some kind along the lines of luncheon vouchers. These could also be used as part of an incentive or reward system, with more vouchers allocated for improved performance.

If you feel that managers will be less than inclined to give people time to visit the centre then perhaps you should investigate their motives. It may be that it is the line manager who requires an incentive to develop his or her staff as well as the individual, so think about addressing the WIIFM (what's in it for me?) factor. Some organizations have a bonus-related system for line managers which is linked to the development of their staff, where improved performance can give them financial rewards or other forms incentive, perhaps in the form of restaurant vouchers. If you are expecting managers to take on increased responsibility then they should be rewarded for it. Alternatively, simply circulate tables of development support within the organization and watch what happens!

Security

With videos costing over £900 a piece, the last thing you want is for them to go walking. It is a difficult balance to obtain, as you want to maintain accessibility but you need to secure these resources. Some centres keep the room locked when it is not in use and others have security passes or codes that need to be entered to access the room. It is definitely worth considering some kind of security for the resources, but don't forget that you need to maintain the balance between having accessibility for the user and piece of mind that the resources are not going to disappear overnight.

Damaged goods

It is always a good idea to have a policy in place before the centre opens for any materials that may go missing or are damaged. Of course your insurance policy will cover a large amount of losses, but you should make individuals responsible for any resources that they damage or lose. Many organizations stipulate that the person using the resources must pay at least a percentage of the value of the resource if it is lost or damaged while in their possession – most people are then more likely to take better care of them and will ensure that the resources are returned on time and in good condition. You may not feel that this is necessary but it is worth considering.

Marketing internally: Finding out what they want

Once you have got the project authorized and you are starting to change the culture you need to start thinking about the marketing process. Once you have done your research and are aware that you do have a market the next step is to address that market and prepare the way.

Changing the culture towards self-development is one thing, what you need to think about now is how you are going to make them aware of the centre. Never underestimate the importance of preparation – if you can excite your audience well in advance it will make things a great deal easier once the centre is open.

One way in which you can do this is simply to involve them from the start. Many organizations have developed questionnaires (see Appendix I for examples) which ask people what they would like the centre to offer. They could also include some of the following questions:

- What do you understand by the term 'open learning centre'?
- How can you see it being of benefit to you?
- What resources would you like to see available?
- What kind of media would you like it to provide – video, book, CBT, CD-ROM?
- When would you use it?
- What if anything might prevent you from using the facility?
- Would you like the opportunity of taking resources away from the centre to use at home?

Learning styles

We are all aware that people have preferred learning styles, and these are often assessed within the context of formal training courses. However, you may want to link these preferences to the resources that you decide to purchase. You may not have access to everyone's learning style so it may be an idea that as part of the questionnaire you ask about learning styles. Or, as part of the awareness process, you could ask line managers to take on this responsibility. You may want to run workshops on developing people, or how they can help people learn, but whatever the mechanism you choose it is worth analysing the responses and using this information to guide you through your product acquisition. If you find that you have a large proportion of Activists and a minimal number of Theorists, you may need to reconsider the volume of text-based resources that you are about to purchase.

Competition time

As with all questionnaires you need to encourage people to complete them, which unfortunately most people are not inclined to do. You know only too well how many times a customer service inventory has been thrown straight into the bin because you haven't got the time to fill it in.

Offer a reward – either a prize or, even better, throw in an element of competition. One idea is to get employees to think of a name and logo for the centre. You may feel that this is not suitable for the culture of your particular organization but you may be surprised – it is not often that people get the chance to be creative and you may find that even those in the most restrictive of roles may have something quite innovative to offer. This will also assist in the sales process, a contribution towards the learning centre will be another step up the ladder.

Set a date for the return of the questionnaires and don't leave it too late. Once you have received them analyse them properly, take on board people's comments and try as much as is possible to respond to them – if they have made the effort then so should you.

Newsletters are a great way of publicizing the project, so use the opportunity to update everyone on the progress the centre is making. If your organization does not produce a newsletter – start one! It is vital not just to leave people hanging. Try to keep them as fully informed as possible – it is after all *their* centre.

Making a corporate video

One way to market the centre is to produce a video which can then be shown to potential users. This is obviously not the cheapest of options, but if you have the funds available it can be a very effective tool. The video can include an initial speech from the managing director, preferably set within the learning centre. This will help sell the centre and will show that there is commitment from the very highest level. If the managing director is unable to participate then get another member of senior management involved. The video could include information about the centre, its purpose, how it can be used, the benefits to the individual user and more logistical information which may include opening hours. If you have the expertise available to you, why not put it in the format of an advertisement – and if you have video conferencing then even better. The video can become an integral part of the induction process, ensuring that people are exposed to their learning responsibilities at the earliest possible opportunity.

Summary

- ■ Use questionnaires to assess needs.
- ■ Hold a competition to name the centre and design the logo.
- ■ Set a deadline for the return of completed questionnaires.
- ■ Publicize the project.
- ■ Keep people updated with your progress.

Chapter 6

Resourcing the Centre

The product mix: How do you decide what to put in it?

The answer to this question really depends on the objective of the learning centre.

- Is it there to complement and support the internal training courses?
- Is it there to help develop employees in line with the competency standards that are in place?
- Have you conducted a thorough needs analysis to find the skill areas that are required for development?

Recent studies conducted by the Industrial Society suggest that the main reason behind the setting up of an organization's learning centre is linked to the spreading of information technology awareness, with 50 per cent of learning centres having this as their main purpose for opening, followed by reference/library system at 42 per cent and multi-skilling at 37 per cent. Various organizations have decided on a mixture of the above, choosing to link the resources with all three, while others have gone for just one solution. Whatever you decide, make sure it is line with the organization's and the individuals' needs.

> Never assume what people will want or need, because you will probably be wrong. You would never dream of putting a series of training courses together without having conducted a thorough needs analysis first, so always ask your potential users.

When you have identified the areas for development, the next step is to think about the type of media that you will be offering. Some organizations' learning centres consist solely of multimedia stations; however, it would seem that most learning centres prefer to provide a mix of media to address everyone's learning styles.

Selecting the media

Your first decision needs to be that of media choice. The media will be the mechanism through which individuals will learn, so you need to spend time thoroughly evaluating the potential usage. The area of multimedia will be discussed in more detail in Chapters 8 and 9. Once you have agreed on the mechanism through which individuals will have the opportunity to learn the next step is choosing your resources.

With thousands of new products being created every year, the training resources market can be a minefield, particularly to those who have not been involved in training, and the cost can come as a horrifying surprise. How do you determine which products are the best ones for your potential users, and which ones are going to meet their needs? Unfortunately the assessment of resources is one area to which people tend to dedicate the least time. Many overstate the importance of cost, continually on the hunt for bargains and best deals, providing a false economy, and potentially leaving themselves with hundreds of products that will simply collect dust on their bookshelves.

> It is all too easy when you are working to a deadline to 'panic buy', so make sure that you allow yourself plenty of time to evaluate resources thoroughly. If you find that you are running out of time then postpone the launch, I admit that this is not an ideal situation, but it is far better to do this than suffer from poor product choice.

You should keep the end user constantly in mind. Your choice will always be a subjective one to a certain degree, but try to detach yourself from the project – you are excited about self-development and open learning, but the end user will initially not be. This is one of the advantages of having a project team or working party with a mixture of training and non-training professionals, as they will be more likely to look at the products from a user's point of view. There has in fact been research on the effectiveness of open learning resources, the result of which suggested that very few organizations dedicate sufficient time to this process and do not seek feedback from their users to ensure that the materials are meeting their needs.

🔑 Key point

One very interesting outcome of this study was that learners preferred materials that were easy to manage and easy to read, and many felt that the materials should have some relevance to their job.

All of this may seem like common sense and not come as any real surprise, but all too often those responsible for acquiring the materials lose sight of the obvious, and as a consequence will have an overstocked and underused learning centre.

Assessing suitability

How do you know if the materials you inspect are going to be suitable? I recently carried out an experiment to see exactly how different groups of individuals would assess the same resources. The experiment involved a wide selection of text-based resources on three different subject areas: teamwork, communication and time management. The materials ranged from heavy, hardback books through workbooks to handy 96-page paperbacks. The first group to assess the material was from the training and human resource department. I allowed them three hours to evaluate the resources and asked them to place what they considered to be good resources for the open learning centre user in one pile. I then repeated this exercise with two other groups – one contained a mix of managers, the other a mix of individuals from all levels of the organization up to line management level.

The results of the experiment proved extremely interesting but predictable – each group had chosen almost entirely different resources. There were some common elements but on the whole some significant differences. The result of this is self-explanatory – we are subjective, and it is difficult to look at materials from a learner's perspective. This is why I feel it is essential to eliminate subjectivity as far as possible by ensuring that a mixed group of individuals are responsible for assessing the materials rather than one individual.

Evaluating the resources

How do you go about this lengthy process of evaluation? Your time can be well spent by using one of the independent facilities provided for evaluation and advice on resources. There are organizations around that can help you (such as independent brokers of training resources) to find the right resources to suit your needs. Many of these organizations' facilities are free of charge, and they provide an invaluable service which will save you an enormous amount of time. Their speciality and knowledge is purely in the field of resources, and they can supply you with a list of possibilities that will match the criteria that you have set for the centre, linking resources to competencies or skill areas that you have identified. Once you have this you can spend days at their centres evaluating the resources.

Make use of these centres, as they will provide you with expert help and guidance. Once you have the list of resources that you need to evaluate, do not attempt to review them all by yourself, but ask colleagues and other managers if they would like to choose areas that they would be interested in evaluating. For example you could ask someone in the marketing department to evaluate four areas and someone from finance to assist you. The advantages of this are enormous, through involving them and valuing their opinion you are increasing the learning centres sales force. And why not include people who you know are particularly sceptical about the whole project? To make the whole process even easier you can supply them with evaluation forms, an example of which is included in Appendix I.

Resources fair

If you find that you do not have the time (or sufficient people) to thoroughly evaluate material there are other options available to you, and one of these is the resource fair. This involves inviting producers/publishers or independent one-stop suppliers to bring a range of resources to your premises. You ensure that everyone in the organization is aware of the event and you invite them along in order that they can see the materials firsthand and provide you with feedback on the resources that they found most useful.

There are several advantages to doing this type of prelaunch affair, the first being that you can stimulate interest in the centre before it opens. You can explain the purpose of the centre and have the opportunity to show people exactly what could be available to them, which provides them with the chance to understand the range of media and to 'have a play'. It will also make them feel part of the project as they will feel that their needs have really been considered. You will of course need to provide them with some kind of evaluation sheet, and this should include some of the following:

- type of resource – audio, video, CD-ROM, CBT, book, workbook, CD-I
- title of product
- reason for choice.

You do not have to ask for personal details of the individual unless you want to analyse who has been to the fair, or you want some kind of report on areas of material for particular departments.

Some organizations have even carried out this kind of event at the launch. They purchase a few resources beforehand, then on the day of the launch they organize for a whole host of other resources to arrive and purchase more based on the feedback gained on the day.

What will your user use?

According to research carried out by the Industrial Society (Training Trends, March 1997) it would appear that the most used resources held within learning centres are videos and books, with audio and laser disk at the bottom of the scale. This could of course be a reflection on the fact that most organizations have a higher proportion of video and text-based material than anything else. What is interesting is the high level of technology usage, particularly in the field of CD-ROM.

How do you know what will work?

You might be the type of person who enjoys reading a comprehensive, theoretical book on time management; the users might well not be. Consider also the time element – people will be using the centre in their own time, and they may not have three hours to go through a package.

☞ Key point

If you are lending out books think about their content – do you really think that people will get around to reading a 400-page business book? And if you are lending material out for a set period is it really feasible that they will be able to read it in that time?

Many of the most successful centres contain resources which are both appealing to the eye and quick and easy to read. This does not mean that the content is weak, there are many books around the 100-page mark which probably contain as much information as one with four times that amount. I am not saying that you should not have anything which is over 100 pages, my point is that you have to ask yourself if you can realistically see someone using the products that you are proposing to purchase.

Summary

- Always keep the end user in mind.
- Spend time evaluating the resources.
- Hold a resources fair.
- Consider different learning styles.

Chapter 7

Types of Resource: What's Available and What Will It Cost?

Workbooks

Most packages these days do come with workbooks, but it is always a good idea to look for additional sources. Workbooks can act as a support mechanism for the other media that you have in place as well as providing an interactive resource that people can take away. These resources also prove very valuable in enabling you to assess the value of the centre in terms of an individual's development, as people will want to see evidence of how skills have improved in the evaluation process. When looking at the suitability of these resources you may want to consider the following.

- How interactive is the workbook?
- Does it contain a good mix of activities and exercises?
- Does it contain case studies?
- Is it well presented?
- How portable is it – ie will it fit comfortably inside a brief-case?

You do not need to buy copies of the workbook for everyone who wishes to use them. Simply ensure that they are aware they must not write inside it, and provide them with exercise books in which they can store their answers.

Audio

The value of audio is greatest to those organizations where many employees spend time out of the office, for example where there is a high proportion of field sales people. There are an increasing number of audios around, not all of which are American in origin. Some of the best material is in the form of an audio book, and many of the popular business classics are now available in this format, for example Covey's *Seven Habits of Highly Effective People* and Blanchard's *One Minute Manager*. This media has another distinct advantage over others in that it is very inexpensive, prices range from as little as £7.99 up to £50, so it is a cost-effective as well as a highly useful way of addressing development needs. The only drawback with this media is that they have a limited shelf life, in that they are not very durable and are easily chewed up in audio players.

You also need to consider the hardware on which you will need to play the audiotapes. Walkmans are often the best mechanism as they allow the individual to listen without disturbing any one else, and are extremely portable.

Video

Linear video has by no means been totally replaced by the advent of multimedia and still remains a valuable resource. If people do not have the time to read a book, or indeed do not enjoy reading, then watching a video can be the ideal solution.

Assessment of these is essential. Try to seek out those which are not from the high profile producers – there is a lot of good material available (which is much cheaper and of excellent quality) from many small producers who simply do not have the marketing budgets to make themselves known. This again is where using an independent resource centre can prove invaluable and also a money-saving exercise. Just because you have never heard of the producer, or because the video is cheap, do not feel that this makes the product unworthy.

When looking at video material it is also worth bearing in mind whether it will be an asset to the learning centre, or whether it is a product that is best kept for a training course.

Humour versus drama

There has been much discussion over the years about the effectiveness of humour within the context of a training video, and it would seem that there are two very distinct arguments. Some believe that humour detracts from the real message that the film is trying to put across, and that delegates will walk away not having properly understood the messages, only remembering the less serious parts of the video and who starred in it. Others are of the belief that people are more likely to retain something if they enjoyed the experience, ie the humour.

Whatever your opinion you need to consider whether the materials will be relevant for use within an open learning environment. Sometimes these films have been produced for the training rather than self-development market and may as a consequence be very trainer led. It is not very often that a video will be used in isolation on a course, and indeed it may be used for a variety of reasons: to create a mood, to provide the trainer with an additional training aid, to show an example of a situation that the trainer cannot explain, or to enable the delegate to empathize with the characters. However, the learning points are very often pulled out by the trainer as opposed to the individuals, so when it comes to evaluating video material for an open learning centre a different approach may need to be taken.

Humorous scenes are often remembered as much for the laughter that occurred from within the dynamics of the group – ie its reaction. If you take this element away from the equation will it be as powerful a learning tool?

Environment

When assessing video-based resources we are often aware of the environment within which they are set, and this often has a bearing on our decision of whether or not to purchase. Not only do we need to ensure that the messages are put across in the correct manner, but we also need to ensure that our delegates will be able to relate to it. How many times on a training course have you heard your delegates state that the video does not apply to them because it is not set in their particular field?

Fortunately we are very often able to overcome these objections in the context of a course, and are able to ensure that the learning points are pulled out regardless of the setting. In an open learning situation this becomes much harder to achieve. As a result when assessing these materials you have much more to consider than you would in an everyday training situation. It may be that the users will not have the ability to extract the messages for themselves, so make sure that the environment is as close to that of their own as possible.

When you are evaluating video material you may want to consider the following:

- Are the learning points easily recognized?
- Will the user be able to relate to it?
- Has the material been designed especially for open learning?
- Will the training department use it?
- Do the messages conflict with the corporate ones?
- Are there visual distractions from the message, ie fashion, if the film is 'old'?
- If it contains legislation, is it up to date?
- Who is it suitable for, and at what level?
- Is there any support material?
- Is it of good quality?
- Is it value for money?

You need to decide whether you will be loaning out the materials. If you are going to do this, it will have a dramatic impact on your choice of media – after all, not everyone will have access to a multimedia station or even a video recorder.

Books: Identifying the bookworms

Books are the most traditional resources held in open learning centres, and have played a part in open learning for many years; however they are certainly not a 'must' now as more options are open to you with the increase in technology. Many OLCs have chosen not to take this route, as is the case at the Atomic Weapons Establishment, where the open learning centre 'ALF' contains only CD-ROM, CBT and CD-I. Most centres do hold a substantial element of text-based resources and, as I have already mentioned, it is always useful to have a range of resources across all media in order that you cater for everyone's needs. However, if you find that your employees are not avid readers, do not invest heavily in this media.

There are numerous advantages to having text-based resources within the centre, they are much cheaper than CD-ROM and video, and address a huge range of development needs. But remember that the resources are there to be used and are not merely decorative items, select them carefully and try to pick a wide selection of styles, as not everyone will want to wade through a 300-page hardback, and in fact most people won't.

There are some first-class books which contain excellent guidance and advice that will only take an individual a few hours to read. For example, Kogan Page's *Better Management* series contains over 60 titles looking at all areas of development from Assertiveness to Office Management and Delegation. Look too at the *Successful in a Week* series from the Institute of Management. These excellent books are nicely laid out with tips and hints on all sorts of issues – these are the books that people will read. The advantage of these kinds of books is that they are quick and easy to understand; the downfall of many business books is that they are bogged down in theory and contain enormous amounts of jargon, which the average manager will have neither the time nor the inclination to digest.

Always try to assess books with the end user in mind – you may understand the terms and concepts contained within certain titles, but will they? This is another advantage of having a project team with a broad base of participants. I am not suggesting that the library contains no heavyweight titles at all, after all some of the users will want theory, and it is important that the library contains a small element of these as they will prove attractive to the senior managers in particular. There are a range of titles that are ideal for this level, mostly the management classics written by the leading gurus, and I have included a list of these in Appendix II.

☞ Key point

Remember that the more weighty the book the longer it will take for it to be read, so you may need to be flexible with your lending times.

Another area to consider is the protection of these books. They will soon become dog eared if you do not protect them, so think about investing in the plastic covers that public libraries use, they are inexpensive and will increase the life span of your valuable resources.

! Tip

You may want to consider purchasing hardback versions of the more popular resources. This will incur extra cost initially but will save you money in the long term.

You may also want to consider linking these resources to the training programmes that are in place, provide the training department with a list of the books that the centre holds and encourage the individual trainers to hand these out to the delegates either before or after courses. This will extend the learning process and provide you with another mechanism through which you can sell the centre.

The other advantage is the service that you will be seen to be providing the training team, reducing any potential conflict that may occur.

Resistance to reading

You may find that there are people who do not enjoy the process of reading and you may come up against the following barriers:

'I don't have time to read.'
'It's boring.'
'It's too much like being at school.'
'I can't concentrate.'
'I can never finish it.'
'I feel selfish when I read.'

If these are some of the reactions that you foresee getting when people see the number of books on your shelves, then suggest that they do not read the whole book. We are perhaps caught in a mind set where we believe that we have to read an entire book to get any value from it. This is very often not the case: there is a lot of value in digesting small chunks at a time.

☛ Key point

Suggest that people read set chapters. It is also worth suggesting that people make notes when reading: there is often a large amount of information to take in, and it would be impossible to expect anyone to understand and digest everything they read without reflecting upon it first. This is perhaps why some of the most successful books advocate going back and reading the chapter again, and include actions and activities that you should conduct to cement what you have acquired by reading, for example Stephen Covey's *Seven Habits of Highly Effective People*.

! Tip

Ask the individual departments to donate some of their books. It will increase the levels of materials in the centre and save you some money!

Chapter 8

Multimedia

Multimedia has been around too long to be termed a fad within the training industry, so it is worth considering quite closely, but what is it and how do I decide whether to go down that route? One major factor in answering this question is ultimately down to the budget that you have for your centre. If you only have a few thousand pounds allocated to resources then CD-ROM is not going to be the best route for you. There are (and I am sure there will continue to be) arguments for and against the use of multimedia – the traditionalist's view claims that people can only learn from text-based resources, and the modernist who will throw all sorts of technical jargon at you, professing that Internet is outdated. I believe that the best learning centres contain a mix of media.

Even if you feel that there really is no place for books you cannot ignore the fact that some people are still very PC shy and prefer a more traditional method. There are all sorts of other factors to consider before you make an investment into multi-media. First, can you afford it? CD-ROM is still not that cheap, the software alone will set you back around £1000 per course, and on top of that you have the cost of the hardware and maintenance. And this is just the initial outlay – as with all media of this nature upgrades will occur and your technology may quickly become outdated, so you have to make sure that you will have the budget to prepare for these changes.

If you do have the resources then you have passed the first obstacle. The second is to think about the needs of the customer. Are you confident that they will use these packages? If, for example, you are in an organization where the technology age is far from prevalent then perhaps you should reconsider and take a more gradual approach. Self-development is one culture change, having a technology change may be more than most can cope with. You also need to identify the leaning styles of the individuals who will be using the centre. If you have a large proportion of Theorists and Reflectors then CD-ROM may not be the ideal solution. Whatever you decide, do not follow this path simply because you feel that everyone else is. Your objective should be to get the centre used – not to be a corporate showroom, and this has been the downfall of far too many learning centres.

As you will see from the case studies in Chapter 13 some of the most successful learning centres have been set up with a small budget and limited resources. The important factor was the enthusiasm and drive behind making it work, not the fancy machinery inside. I may have put technology-based training in a negative light – this is not my intention as I am a strong believer in its value, but you do need to ensure that it is right for your organization first. Multimedia has many advantages, particularly in the selling stage of the centre. It can act as a great incentive to get people in.

🔑 Key point

Many people are worried that their children know more about technology than they do and are desperate to catch up. The learning centre can provide them with this opportunity. You can also take advantage of the change in the culture over the last few years where many managers are now expected to use and understand technology. The demise of the personal secretary has left many managers feeling uncertain and almost embarrassed about their lack of knowledge in this field – and with the information age really taking off, most senior managers are expected to have an awareness of multimedia and its uses. These are the issues that you need to attack and having multimedia can provide you with a great weapon to be used to your advantage.

Another great advantage of multimedia is without a doubt the interaction and support that it provides for the learner. Training has moved away from the chalk and talk classroom days; we know that people learn best through experiencing situations and enjoying them, so why should open learning be any different? Going through a CD-ROM package enables people to learn at their own pace, and, if they don't understand first time around they can go back and there is no one else around to belittle them. It can be a personal experience in a very non-threatening environment. Of course there will always be those who prefer to read or to attend a course, but multimedia can provide great support.

There are other things that you need to consider before taking the plunge, such as the software. Many producers have been quick to identify the market, particularly within open learning centres, and packages are being produced daily, many of which are unfortunately overpriced and of a very poor standard. You need to shop around, or go to an independent adviser who will guide you towards the best and most cost-effective packages on the market. Do not cut costs – if there is a free hardware offer do not buy ten packages simply because you may get a thousand pounds worth of equipment free. It will not be a wise investment in the long run, particularly if the majority of packages are not being used.

There are some excellent packages available that have been produced by small organizations, so do not just opt for the higher profile organizations. There is some excellent material available at a lower cost which is just as effective.

! Tip

Seek independent advice – it does not cost you anything and it could save you a small fortune in the long run.

CD-I versus CD-ROM

The question 'which is better, CD-ROM or CD-I?' is one which people have been posing for a long time; unfortunately it is not an easy question to answer. Many people want to make a choice between the two media as they see them as similar. This is not the case – they are both very different and so are the individual merits of both. Compact Disk Interactive (CD-I) has been around for several years now with products first being developed by Phillips. CD-I, unlike CD-ROM, runs through a television screen, and is connected to a player which resembles a video recorder. The packages are on disk exactly like ROM and are controlled by the user through the use of a joystick or mouse attachment.

CD-I was initially designed not purely for open learning and self-study, but to provide an interactive mechanism within a more traditional training environment, and this dual function is really what separates it from CD-ROM. The initial packages produced by Phillips took the format of graphics rather than the full motion video which appears in the new products available from video producers. Some people feel that CD-I was simply an experimental product paving the way for more advanced technology, acting purely as a transitional media which primed people for the use of other interactive systems. The same view was also held with regard to laser disk; however, this does not explain why many learning centres have achieved great success with both media running side by side.

The benefits of CD-I

The Royal Marsden Hospital NHS Trust, which has recently opened two learning centres, has invested in both media and quickly seen the benefits of CD-I, believing that it is 'a valuable mechanism for self-paced learning because it engages and involves the user'. It has also taken advantage of its dual function, with the packages being used by managers on the wards and in departments to conduct small group training sessions. The advantages of CD-I are quite distinct: they provide full motion media on the whole screen as opposed to a small element, they are extremely user friendly and are welcomed by those who suffer from technophobia. They can also be utilized within a group situation which is very difficult to do with a CD-ROM. The hardware itself is also less expensive than a multimedia station, and much easier to maintain.

The future of CD-I

CD-I may not be a media that you want to invest in heavily, but it is certainly worth considering as an additional mechanism. It is extremely portable, which means that it can be loaned out to an individual if requested, and team leaders can use it to facilitate sessions with relative ease. It is difficult to say, as with any technology, whether this is the one that will soon be antiquated, but then if we keep thinking of the dinosaur issue, we could foresee that the Internet will be superseded within the next three years. This is why it is important to ensure that not only do you have adequate funds to set up the centre, but that you will have continuing funds to support it. Think of the needs of the users as they are now but just as importantly look a year ahead, beyond that you cannot predict what will and what will not be outdated.

! Tip

The key to your choice of media is to make sure that *you* understand it. If this means attending a training course then so be it; if you expect your customers to be able to use it then you must be in a position to show them how.

Revolving libraries

Once you have decided on the path that you wish to take as far as media is concerned then you need to think about the packages to invest in. As these will probably take up the majority of your resources budget it is worth investing time in the evaluation process. As learning centres become more prevalent and the use of multimedia increases so too does the availability of resources – producers have found a new market and a big market, and they want you to buy their products. So, which ones are the best, and how do you evaluate them?

There are currently three major players in the CD-ROM production field:

1. Training Direct (Longman as was)
2. Xebec
3. Tarragon.

However it is worth repeating that there are many other smaller organizations who have developed excellent packages and this is again where an independent resource centre can prove invaluable. As these products are expensive to purchase you may want to consider a library option. This means that for a upfront payment you can have access to a number of packages throughout the year that you can then return and swap for new ones. This system has great advantages: it allows you to have access to new resources, which you can market to your customers; it also means that when you have a new initiative in place you can keep the product until the demand dies down, which in turn means that you are not left with dusty product lying on the shelf.

It has been suggested that introverts are more likely to make use of the learning centre than extroverts, which may be down to the fact that learning centres are places in which individuals work on their own with little need to interact with anyone other than a PC. If this is true then you need to ensure that the materials you have are good enough to encourage the loudest of extroverts – try to make them aware that the learning centre is not a traditional library, they are allowed to talk and drink coffee etc. (although it would appear from recent reports that traditional public libraries are also suffering a major culture change and are trying desperately to shed the dusty image that they have created over the years).

Computer-based training (CBT)

CBT packages have been around for years and you may think that it would be a step backwards to invest in them; but it would be a great shame if you did not evaluate some of the packages that are currently around. CBT has distinct advantages in the role of open learning; apart from being much cheaper, it is user friendly, portable and therefore easy to loan out. If you have invested in the hardware for multimedia then the investment is relatively minimal as far as CBT is concerned. The graphics may not be as glossy as those on CD-ROM, but the benefits to the user are the same. Research recently carried out by CBT systems showed that computer-based training now accounts for between 20 per cent and 100 per cent of companies' overall training programmes and it is estimated that it will continue to grow at an annual rate of 35 per cent.

The use of CBT in these statistics largely represents the field of computer software training, which is good news for open learning centres. If people are getting into the habit of self-development, in whatever area, it means that they will already be used to the process and learning from their desk or from a learning centre is becoming part of their culture. As the development of technology increases and more organizations change to software packages, the need to train people in its use increases. CBT provides a cost-effective mechanism in which people can learn at their own pace in their own time. It also takes the pressure away from the IT department, with individuals gaining access to self-development resources that will help them solve their problems.

 # Key point

Having IT resources available within your centre will you give a distinct advantage over those that do not. Many of the organizations that have these resources within their centre have clearly stated that they have been a large contributory factor to its success. So if your organization is installing new software make sure that you have the resources in your centre for people to access it. Include basic PC skills training too, as well as touch-typing courses and multimedia awareness programmes. These materials need not be expensive – CBT courses can start from as little as £50 and there are also some excellent text-based resources around.

Self-diagnostics

Another point worth mentioning with regard to CBT materials are the packages that allow an individual to assess their own areas of need. Some organizations have made such packages available on a stand-alone PC within a staff restaurant, as it is much easier for someone to identify their own need than it is for someone else to point out an area of development for them.

There are some excellent packages around that provide the user with an opportunity to test all sorts of skills, from time management to grammar and delegation skills. If you can provide individuals with a relatively quick and easy way of identifying development needs then they may be more likely to attend to those and will use the centre as a mechanism through which to do so. These packages would by no means replicate any other form of needs analysis but will allow users to identify their own skill gaps that had not already been identified through any other medium.

Chapter 9

Non-vocational Materials

Is there a need?

It is the policy of many organizations not to have non-vocational materials within the learning centre. If the organization is investing heavily in the development of the centre it is because it wants the users to develop themselves in line with the organization's objectives. This is a very upsetting approach to a resource centre and one which we come across all too frequently.

Part of the resistance to the learning centre from the users' perspective is that they feel that the organization is cutting costs, and they are not encouraged to attend training courses because that may mean two days away from their desks, whereas they can absorb the same amount of information from a course by going to the learning centre in their lunch hour. If the centre has nothing but material to develop the individual in terms of business skills then this will only help to reinforce this opinion, and you may find you have a lot of resentment when the centre opens. We feel that the inclusion of non-vocational material is invaluable.

The objective of a learning centre should be (in my opinion) to assist and support an individual in their own development, helping them to realize their whole potential. This does not mean turn them into a machine, but to help them understand where their own strengths and weaknesses lie, and to take the opportunity to help them develop these learning opportunities. To reiterate, because I do not feel this point can ever be overstated, it is not a natural process, particularly in our society, to take the initiative to learn through our own means. How many of us have taken up new sports or social activities in the last year, whether at colleges, in the evenings or at weekends? Very few I would imagine. It takes a lot of self-motivation to set time aside for our own personal development, particularly with all the continuing pressures of organizations restructuring, new technology and systems, lack of time or family commitments. It is not an enviable task to ask someone to devote some of this precious time to enhance their time management skills in the OLC at 5 o'clock at night when all they want to do is get home. Part of this process can be facilitated by offering resources that will be of a personal benefit and these should be advertised.

Parlez-vous Français?

One area to focus on is the inclusion of language resources, not least because the most popular courses taken up at evening classes across the country are those of languages. Many organizations such as Zeneca Pharmaceuticals offer employees the opportunity to attend language classes held at their training centre, which is also home to their open learning centre. If people are dedicating more of their own time to the organization by working long hours then shouldn't we be offering them something in return? The cost of language resources is relatively inexpensive when you consider that the cost of a CD-ROM can be as little as £99, yet the benefits are enormous. Having these resources will stimulate interest within the centre and will tempt people towards other resources; you want to get people into the centre and this is one of the methods that can help you achieve this. It will also curb some of the resistance to the centre, with individuals feeling that there is actually something there for their own personal needs. Other organizations such as London Ambulance Service (see case study, page 142) have gone one step further and have resources that cover more personal interests such as cookery and sport, and even have a CD-ROM on learning to drive! All of these products have helped them develop an interest in the centre which is certainly reflected in their usage figures.

If you do decide to include resources of this nature then try to restrict them to the more popular areas of general interest, otherwise you will be receiving requests to include resources on anything from astronomy to cross-stitch made easy. Other areas of inclusion regarding non-vocational material might be:

- planning a wedding
- world history
- home furnishing
- sport
- cookery
- general health and well-being.

Career development

We have considered the value of the centre containing non-vocational materials (languages, cookery etc), but have you thought about the value of holding material that will be of direct value to the individual in terms of career progression? With so many organizations 'restructuring' or 'downsizing' (whatever term you feel happier with) the need is becoming greater to provide resources of this nature that will help individuals in their search for a new career. There are a whole host of areas that this can cover, for example:

- writing your CV
- interview techniques
- career planning
- setting up your own business
- self-esteem
- surviving the restructuring process.

These materials will not only add to the resources that you currently hold but will eliminate the feeling that the centre is only there to train and improve people's capability in their existing roles, rather than to assist them as individuals. If your organization really wants to invest in people then providing materials of this nature is an absolute must.

The Internet: Does it have a place in the learning centre?

As more and more organizations go online, the role of the Internet becomes increasingly important to our business culture, and it may therefore be worth considering having access within the learning centre. It may even be a good idea to offer this facility for those centres that have a very minimal budget, as the cost of the Internet is relatively small yet the access to information is huge.

The Internet was originally designed as an exchange medium, primarily for academic purposes. Individuals were able to gain access to a wide range of information from all over the world, cutting out the time they would normally have to spend contacting various institutions for documentation. It has now evolved into a selling mechanism as well as an information exchange, in which anything and everything can be accessed – you can buy stocks or fine wines, and get information on anything from rollerblading to the latest research on the sea-horse.

All you need to gain access to the Internet is a computer which has a presence on the net, a modem and an account with an Internet service provider. The cost is relatively minimal, as you can choose to pay per month and have unlimited access, or per call. It is up to you to decide which option is going to be the most cost effective. There are all sorts of packages available on the market so it is definitely worth shopping around for the best deal.

Cybercafé

If you want to get people into your centre and feel that you need a sweetener to entice them in, then the Internet can provide the ideal solution. You may well have seen the recent surge in so-called cybercafés – bars that have PCs linked to the Internet. They offer the general public the chance to 'surf' the net – and by providing this opportunity they are enticing people into *their* bars as opposed to their competitors', a great marketing ploy, and one that does not have to be restricted to a bar. Why not use the same tactic for your learning centre? A cybercafé may well prove the ideal solution for those centres that are committed to personal development but that do not have large funds to purchase large amounts of resources.

The other advantage is the move towards the change in culture – many people have an interest in the Internet and would be more than happy to have the opportunity to see exactly how it functions. It also provides people with the opportunity to gain access to a wealth of information that they may not normally have access to. And finally, it increases the opportunity for people to take responsibility for their own development rather than this being something they have 'done' to them.

The dangers

If you do decide to include an Internet facility, ensure that people are aware of the costs involved, particularly if you are paying per call rather than a standard monthly charge as it could become very expensive. It is wise to restrict the facility to a stand-alone computer rather than use a network. You also need to ensure that the PC on which you want to access is sufficiently powerful – the last thing you want is to entice people to the centre to make use of the facility only to find that they need half an hour to access a couple of pages.

Alternative media: Games and activities

You need not be restricted to the more traditional forms of media, for example you may want to consider incorporating games and activity-based resources into the centre and there are two very good reasons for doing this. First, you may be getting a certain degree of resistance from the training department who feel concerned that with everyone developing themselves they will soon be out of a job! By incorporating games and other trainer-led materials you are encouraging the trainers to make use of the centre, and to see the benefits hands on.

Second, you are encouraging managers and coaches to take responsibility for their staff's development by providing them with the tools with which to do so. Games can assist a line manager with a whole range of development issues: they can use them at team briefings, have them at their disposal when they need to run a team-building session, or when someone needs to liven up an annual conference. And remember interactive games can be used by individuals.

🗝 Key point

There is a large selection of management exercises that lend themselves to being used by one person. For example, one particular organization has had great success with the development of a series of action maze exercises across a range of issues, including: absenteeism, negotiation, people problems, customer care and health and safety. These mazes are a little like playing 'Dungeons and Dragons' – they provide the individual with a situation, they then have to select an appropriate response which then elicits the outcome and so they are provided with the next scenario. People find these kinds of exercises extremely useful because they are forced to put themselves into a certain situation and are asked 'what would you do if...?'

There are hundreds of others, but one which has been particularly successful in learning centres has been a behavioural and interpersonal skills board game called 'Win Win'. This game contains hundreds of role plays, mimes and situations that the individual is asked to enact, these can either be done as an individual or in pairs. This particular game has been known to get itself into staff restaurants on more than one occasion.

When looking at these kinds of resources for the centre choose ones which you feel can be used by several people in the organization, and try to look for those which contain a substantial amount of flexibility.

 ## Key point

Team-building games are always popular as they are multipurpose. Communication is another area worth looking at. It may well be that you do not need to purchase any games or activities at all – try negotiating with the training department, as they may have some they would be more than happy to donate.

Health and safety

Health and safety materials are a good addition to any learning centre, not least to ensure that you will increase your usage figures by at least one person – the health and safety officer. They also prove useful for induction purposes and increasingly so for line managers. They need not be costly, as by tradition health and safety materials have always been a lot cheaper than their management development counterparts. There are materials available across a wide range of media too, from CD-ROM and CD-I to workbooks and action mazes as previously mentioned.

If you do decide to dedicate a section to health and safety, it is best to stick to the more general areas such as general office safety, fire, manual handling, personal protective equipment, cost and risk assessment. However, general office safety should be sufficient for most. If you go into heath and safety law you will need to ensure that the products you have are in keeping with current legislation, and this may mean that you need to set money aside to keep abreast of new developments in this area.

Professional qualifications

If individuals within your organization are obliged to undertake professional qualifications then you should include some of the recommended textbooks – you can then guarantee that individuals will find a need for the centre. If you do not want to purchase them ask each of the relevant departments if you can put some of their resources into your library – they may of course be less than willing but it is certainly worth a try. You may also want to include resources that will help individuals achieve personal qualifications, eg MBAs.

Journals and periodicals

Subscribing to some of the key periodicals and journals can be a great stimulator, some centres even have daily papers for people to read. This will attract the early starters, who after reading the paper will almost certainly browse at all the other resources on offer. Your biggest battle is to get people into the centre, and any method that will encourage people to use the centre is a bonus. Try to get people to come to the centre as a matter of habit – if they come in every day to read the paper, every month to see the latest journal, or once a year to brush up on their French before their holiday, all this is going to stimulate the culture change.

Resources to develop study skills

As the key to running a successful centre is the creation of a learning environment, created by a change in attitude towards the way in which people develop, it is useful to provide individuals with the tools that will enable them to do this. Many of the potential users may not have undertaken any formal study for a number of years and may have forgotten how to study and to learn. It is always worth investing in a few products that will not only enable others to learn but will also help managers to develop their staff.

There are some great resources around across a wide range of media. Peter Honey has developed some excellent materials for this very purpose, for example 'How to use your learning styles' and the 'Learning log' are very inexpensive items, both under £10, and will enable the user to understand exactly how they can learn. There are also other materials which look at planning your own development and guides to study which will prove invaluable to any potential user. See Appendix II for recommended resources.

Senior management resources

There is a distinct shortage in quality resources for senior managers. Some resources link to generic skills applicable for all levels, for example communication, interpersonal skills and IT, but what about the more strategic elements? Getting the senior managers to use the centre may well be a difficult hurdle but one which you should certainly try to overcome, even though many senior managers may be of the opinion that the reason they are in that position is because they do not have any learning needs, and would most certainly not be seen reading a book on assertiveness amid the masses.

Of course not all senior managers can be tarred with the same brush and one cannot generalize, but you should be prepared for this reaction as it is not uncommon. How do you get the senior managers to use the centre? Some organizations allocate times when the centre is open purely for the use of the senior management team. I personally do not approve of this kind of segregation (especially when organizations are becoming so-called flat and empowered), because it takes you back to the days of separate dining facilities, which I know are still prevalent. But the objective is to get the centre used, and if this is the only way in which you can entice senior managers to do so then it may be the only option. Going back to the question of resources, it is important to ensure that there are materials that the senior managers will use, ie they must be of the correct pedigree and, for example, include case studies.

> Try to include best-selling titles from key gurus like Tom Peters, Pascale, Moss Kanter, Clutterbuck and Handy. And keep them updated. Make sure that as soon as Peters latest book comes out the centre has it, and publicize this fact.

There are all sorts of resources around for senior managers if you look, and again you could refer to an independent body to help you locate them. Another way of getting the senior team interested is to hold a technology awareness workshop for them in the learning centre. Many will not want to display their lack of knowledge in this field and would welcome the chance to gain some ground knowledge in a relatively safe and non-threatening environment. You could also arrange breakfast discussions to entice them in, arrange for some keynote speakers to come in to the centre and talk about relevant issues for a couple of hours, and try to link this if possible to self-development and learning within organizations. You will of course have to pay for this privilege but it will definitely be worthwhile.

Chapter 10

Logistics

―――――――

Cataloguing the material

Now that you have decided what to purchase and in what format, the next stage is to make the purchase – ensure that you negotiate the best deals possible from each of the producers as you will often be given a discount on bulk purchases. Even better, go to an independent resource centre. Many organizations make use of this facility and, once they have been given independent advice, place their order for the resources through them, giving them the responsibility of negotiating the best deals on their behalf. It also means that you can order everything from one supplier, which should make your life a lot easier, allowing you to devote time to your marketing plans etc.

Once all the material has arrived, at least three weeks before your launch you need to start cataloguing it. Different organizations do this in different ways. The main thing to ensure is that it will be visually enticing to the customer, as well as being easy to locate individual products, both for you and the customer – the last thing you want is to be searching for half an hour for that book on change management. Make sure that whatever system you decide to adopt is consistent, ie do not put some things into alphabetical order by title and others by author, as this will end up confusing you and your customer.

Make it simple; many centres have colour coding systems, different coloured dots representing different competencies that the product relates to or the skill area. Of course, you cannot simply rely on colours, you will need either a bar coding or numbering system. Bar coding has been used for many years within public libraries and is an extremely effective way of maintaining the whereabouts of your resources. It is more expensive than the standard labels but much more effective for a large centre. Keep it simple: use V for video followed by a number, B for book and so on. Keep all the resources together that relate to a specific issue, it will then be much easier for you and the customer to locate the correct material.

Once you have physically catalogued the materials you should keep a note of them, either in a hard copy format or on some sort of database. If you do not have one internally, there are a couple that have been designed specifically for use in a learning centre environment. It is extremely important that a good administration system in place from the outset. If you want to put across a professional image then having the right systems is a must.

You will need to keep track of all the materials that are sent out. Too many centres end up wasting resources simply because they cannot keep track of those that have been sent out. If you do not want to be included in these then sort your system out now and stick to it.

Chapter 11

The Launch

With any product, once the market has been identified, the product developed and marketing has commenced, there is always a formal launch. This gives people both the opportunity to see exactly what you have been doing over the last few months and a taste of what they can have access to in the future. But what do you do? Launches vary from organization to organization depending on the budget that is available at the time. Some are all-singing, all-dancing affairs with celebrities cutting the ribbon, while others are nothing more than a few curly sandwiches and sausages on a stick at lunchtime.

The vital key is that it need not be a costly exercise to be a success. You need to set objectives for the launch of the centre – what do you want it to achieve? What will be its purpose? If it is to sell the idea of the centre to employees then it needs to be a smooth and professionally planned day.

A launch can be anything from a lunchtime gathering to a whole-day affair. Some organizations have planned full-day launches that are more like workshops; these have been very successful, with games and competitions being held throughout the day. The idea of competitions within the launch is not as banal as it may seem. Not everyone will want to give up their precious lunch hour to come and visit your centre, so it is up to you to entice them. Why do you think all the best publicized events offer free wine? It certainly is not a mere philanthropic gesture; it is because they realize that most us love a freebie! I am not necessarily suggesting alcohol as a means of getting them along, but you can offer some very good alternatives.

Think about things that would make you give up *your* time. Competitions are an excellent medium, due to the usual amount of competitiveness prevalent among most organizations. Some that we have organized have been targeted at different departments, with the winner earning a prize not usually connected to self-development, but more of a personal reward – a meal out or a bottle of champagne – use your imagination. It does not matter if the competition does not necessarily revolve around traditional open learning.

The objective of the launch is to get people into the centre and to provide them with the opportunity to 'play' with the different types of media. Many will have their own mindset about open learning, linking it back to bad school-day memories of thick and uninspiring text books; some may not have opened a book for several years, let alone used a CD-ROM or CD-I machine.

The launch is your opportunity to sell the centre and to sell the idea of self-development, so let them see that it can be a fun and non-threatening thing to do. Many of the CD-I packages and CD-ROMs include some kind of test – get them to complete them in groups, the winner has the highest score – but keep it basic, you do not want to frighten people off.

Or make up a kind of treasure hunt, ask people to answer a series of questions – the responses will be hidden in some of the packages in the learning centre. There are all kinds of things you can do, the key is to make it fun. We have had civil servants building cars out of plastic tubes on launches that we have organized, so in terms of activity the sky really is the limit, and you will be surprised by the response that you get.

Competitions are only one element of the launch; a successful launch should be planned well in advance of the opening. It does not matter if you do not meet the date that you set yourself for opening, but once you have informed everyone of the date of the launch then it really is vital that you aim to achieve it. If you fail the centre will lose credibility before it has even opened. You have a hard enough job ahead of you once it is up and running, and such attitudes at the beginning could really impede you. Once you have the date you need to inform everyone. You need to decide who you want to invite (will it be all employees or just a select few?) or, as in the case of some organizations, do you want to organize two launches, one for senior staff and another for everyone else? These are things that you need to think about well in advance of the launch. There really is no best standard format but there are key principles that are worth considering.

- Give people plenty of notice.
- Be on hand to answer any questions.
- If you have produced a catalogue, hand it out.
- Ask for feedback and listen to it.
- Ensure that at least one member of the senior management team attends.
- Organize a competition or two.
- Keep a log of all those who attended.
- Make sure they come back.

If you do decide to invite everyone check first with line managers, to ensure that they will allow their staff time to visit the centre. It is better to have a whole-day event, as you are more likely to get a greater attendance if people do not have to dedicate their own time. Once this has been agreed, look on it as a true launch; if you can show people that it is a serious affair from the start your life will be made a lot easier. Use your 'champions' to promote it for you, and design an invitation that can be mailed out to all employees. The invitation could include a brief explanation of what the open learning centre is and how it works.

> You are cordially invited to the official opening ceremony
> of the learning centre to be held on the 24th November at
> 10pm in the Training Suite.
>
> RSVP

If you do decide to hold a competition, make sure that you include this information on the invitation, and if you are lucky enough to have the available resources for a celebrity make sure the invitees know about it. If you decide to offer a free lunch, tell them! You don't have to use just a traditional invitation, use e-mail, video conferencing, any way of communication you can think of, and in this instance there is no such thing as overkill. Once people know where it is and when it is they are more likely to come and see what it is all about.

One organization went so far as to hire actors dressed as schoolmasters to roam their premises to remind people of the launch. This is one unique example, but the point is made. Try and get a senior manager, or if at all possible the MD, to advocate the launch. Get them to put a general memorandum out stating the importance of self-development and how they would greatly appreciate the support of all staff in the launch of the centre.

Promotional materials

It is always a good idea to offer freebies to entice people to attend. These can include anything from promotional pens with the logo of the centre and telephone number, to T-shirts and sweat shirts. Again it us up to you to let your creativity run wild. This may seem like a pointless exercise but remember the most important thing for you is to get people through that door, and often a little bribery can work wonders. As long as it works, what does it matter?

! Tip

Have promotional mouse mats printed with details of the learning centre.

Celebrities

As I mentioned earlier some organizations have invited key/ significant speakers along to the launch of the centre, again to act as a mechanism to get people to attend, and if you have the budget this is a good idea. The term 'celebrity' does not mean that you need to invite a member of the royal family or someone from a popular soap opera, some organizations have invited people who are well known within their industry – actors from training films or even robots, as was the case with Mercury Communications, whose truly 'party'-like launch was attended by 'Adam', the robot from the Longman training video 'Safe Working With VDUs'. Most launches are attended by the managing director or chairman of the organization, and this is one of the best selling points you can ever hope to achieve. If employees can see that the MD really has taken an interest in the centre they are less likely to question its merit (unless, of course, they do not value him or her, but that is another issue altogether).

Cutting the ribbon

Once the centre has been formally opened you need to set the agenda for the remainder of the day – do you want a formal or informal affair with people drifting in throughout the day? Whatever you decide it is imperative that there is someone from the team present at all times to ensure that someone is available to answer any questions that people may have. The centre, and all your efforts, will quickly lose credibility if this is not the case.

Many launches have included formal presentations on the centre and the types of media that are contained within it. I think this may put people off, and suggest a much more relaxed approach, allowing people to wander around and absorb, but you should talk to people, find out what they think, what they do and do not like about the centre. Was it what they expected? Did it meet their expectations and if not why not? What would they like to see in the centre? Make the most of the launch as it is your opportunity to get some great feedback as well as to sell it.

Checklist

☐ Will the launch be an all-day affair?
☐ Who will be invited?
☐ How will you promote it?
☐ Will people be released during the working day?
☐ Who will officially open the centre?
☐ How will you assess people's reactions to it?
☐ Will you provide catering?
☐ What promotional material will you have available?
☐ What competitions will you organize?

Feedback: What did they think?

Looking a little closer at feedback, it is worth noting that the launch does provide you with an opportunity to find out what people really think. After all your hard work try not to be too defensive about your accomplishment, accept positive criticism, if people can see that there is room for movement and flexibility they are more likely to come back. There are of course different ways of obtaining feedback, and if you are involved in training you will know exactly how to do this. Some organizations have prepared questionnaires which are dished out to people on their way out – a 'happy sheet' you might say. The value of this method has been criticized and discussed for a long time, and this will continue for a long time yet, but I still believe that, although it may not give you an exact representation of people's feelings, it does act as a good indicator of them. We all know that people are likely to leave on a high and as a consequence are more likely to think that the centre was fantastic, but we also know that if they did not like it then you will soon find out.

Another problem that trainers will be familiar with is the lack of returned questionnaires. Again, bribery is your best bet – offer a prize draw. Put a number at the bottom of the questionnaire and from those that are returned and completed pick a winner – a simple idea but one that has proved extremely valuable in the past. You may even decide to use a suggestion box to gain ideas and feedback – it may be old fashioned but it is effective. Do not ignore the ideas and suggestions that are put forward, no matter how ridiculous or obscure; make sure that people know that you are taking this seriously, so respond to them. It may be that they still do not understand what the learning centre is all about, and you should look upon it as an opportunity to get someone else into the net.

Remind yourself the centre is a shop, you have products and now you need customers, otherwise it is going to fail! Examples of an evaluation questionnaire can be found in Appendix I.

! Tip

The launch does not have to be a one-off. If it worked, you can do it again, once a year, quarterly, or to coincide with seasonal holidays such as Christmas, Easter etc.

Checklist

☐   What is the objective of the launch?
☐   What do you want to achieve?
☐   How will you promote it?
☐   How long it will last?
☐   Who will you invite?
☐   What will the format of the day be?
☐   How will you evaluate the success of the launch?

Launch programme ideas

- Competitions
- Finance for non-financial managers' quiz – 'Figure it Out' CD-I
- 'Ideas into Action' – CD-I package
- MTA Kit – Construct a 4-wheeled vehicle in five minutes (team-based)
- Action maze competitions
- Building blocks.

Chapter 12

Administration and Logistics

Evaluation methods

Feedback sheets

One of the most important aspects of your role will be to provide those paying for the learning centre with some form of evaluation, in order that they can see exactly where the organization's money is being spent, and indeed if it is being spent wisely. You will of course need to provide them with financial information, but they will also need and want to see the returns for the initial outlay. This is probably the most difficult part of any learning centre manager's role.

As with more traditional forms of training, it is very difficult to show tangible and instantaneous results of the learning centre, so how can its effectiveness be measured in order to provide this kind of information? There are many ways of achieving this, one being to obtain as much feedback as possible from the users, and as with training this can be done by using feedback sheets. They might not provide a completely accurate view of the effectiveness of the centre, but they will provide you with some indication of its value to the users. Ensure that everyone who uses the centre completes an evaluation form; the sorts of areas that it may incorporate are:

- general appearance of the centre
- layout of resources
- mix of material
- induction process.

The sorts of questions that should be asked are:

- Did the materials meet the individual's needs?
- How easy was the media to use?
- How easy were the resources to locate?
- How conducive to learning did you find the centre?
- What other areas would you like to see covered within the learning centre?

Try not to get carried away with the questionnaire – an initial form of feedback such as this need only be quite short, you are only requesting initial reactions.

Other forms of measurement need to be carried out away from the learning centre. Ask the individual's managers if they have seen a noticeable improvement in the way in which a member of staff is working – ask them to provide you with feedback. Do not attempt to do it all yourself, you simply will not have the time. Some administration packages include some form of evaluation/review mechanism, they can even provide you with details of those users who have not completed the forms. (See Appendix IV for a sample screen.)

Evaluating usage

Feedback sheets will give you some indication of the success of the centre, but as I mentioned earlier you will probably need to have access to much more detailed analysis. Before the centre is open you should start to think about the sort of information that you will want to tap into, this will then enable you to ensure that you have the correct and efficient reporting mechanisms available. There is a list of some of the information that you may need to provide:

- details of resources used on a monthly/daily basis
- a breakdown of the most popular media used
- the most popular resource
- numbers of people using the centre
- analysis of departmental usage
- times when the centre is used most/least
- number of resources sent out on loan
- average number of days products are sent out
- reasons for use, eg self-development, supplement training course, non-vocational
- analysis of usage based on level within the organization.

These are just a few of the reports that you may wish to generate; however, there may be more that your organization may request that have not been detailed. You may not feel that this degree of analysis is necessary and you may even think that it will prove extremely time consuming. However, if you do not analyse and monitor the usage correctly you will soon find that the centre is not meeting the needs of your customers and its usage will rapidly start to drop. If you are aware that the marketing department, for example, is using the centre least, you can do something about it immediately and can target them specifically, and if you are aware that some products are more popular than others, you can justify purchasing additional copies.

You may be asking yourself how you can generate these reports without spending hours analysing the figures. There are several options open to you which are discussed in the next section.

The manager's role in the evaluation process

Do not take on unnecessary responsibility as far as the evaluation process is concerned; you will have more than enough to do simply by ensuring that the centre is running efficiently and is being used. It is only possible to provide a limited amount of evaluation in terms of the effectiveness of the centre in an individual's development, and the most efficient way of obtaining more of this kind of information is to ask the line managers to get involved. This also increases their own awareness of the development needs of their staff. Give them a list of resources that their staff have used within the learning centre and ask them to provide you with any marked improvement in that individual's level of competency. It is part of their role to assess this for future appraisal etc, so make sure that they are involved from as early a stage as possible.

Information systems

Due to the increase in the move towards learning centres, not only have producers and publishers been busy developing material to meet the needs of the market, but so too have IT producers, and while there is still a huge gap in the market for good quality management systems, there are some in existence that are being used successfully within the open learning centre market. One which we developed, called 'Resource manager', is a complete management system designed specifically for use only within the learning centre environment. This resource is detailed in Appendix VI.

The learning centre catalogue

Now that you have the systems in place and the product in the centre the next step is to think about how you are going to make people aware of the products that you have. The catalogue is your main selling tool, apart from yourself that is, so it is important that time and money (to a certain extent) are spent on ensuring that it is absolutely right. Think about what you want your catalogue to achieve, and spend time having a look at some you already have. What sort of format do you find most appealing? Does a long list of resources in no particular order really inspire you? I doubt it – you need not spend a fortune, as some organizations have on creating an all-singing, all-dancing catalogue, as its importance lies really in the initial stages. You will probably find that few people will refer to it and will simply ring you and ask what you have on certain issues, but it does act as a good marketing tool and point of reference so it should never be overlooked, and is vital in the beginning.

How do you go about producing it? What should it look like and how much information does it need to contain? Some organizations have outdone themselves by putting their catalogue into unique formats; one organization handed out over 30,000 Filofaxes to each member of staff containing an index of all the resources available to them. Not an inexpensive procedure as I am sure you can imagine, and the company actually withdrew them after the first year realizing that the exercise had been costly and ultimately ineffective. They have now adopted a different approach and have taken a leaf from the producers' catalogue, and their catalogue now contains colour images of some of the material that the centre contains. It has been very well planned and is extremely user friendly, with an index at the front, and each of the sections is linked to the competencies that the organization has in place. There is also a glossary which explains the terminology used and there are useful references to learning style suitability. Its glossiness is not its appeal, although I am sure it helps, but what makes it a success is that it has been well thought-out with the end user clearly in mind at all times. Each of the products also contains a 50-word synopsis of the key learning points of each product, books contain reference to the author, date and number of pages, while videos and CD-ROMs contain details on study time and date of production. (I have included some sample styles of catalogue pages in Appendix III for readers who would like some ideas on format.)

Some catalogues also include generic order forms that can be photocopied and faxed to the learning centre, in order that the individual can request material, this works particularly well when you have branch locations. You may also want to include more general information on the learning centre, outlining contact numbers and names, opening hours, how the centre works and lending facilities and timescales. It may also be an idea to include a list of the training courses that are being run that year and this could either be in a completely separate section or linked to each of the relevant skill areas.

Once you have decided upon the format of the catalogue and have included all the resources you need to make it available to the users. It is up to you how you do this; some organizations have made it available to all employees, others to departments, but whatever you decide make sure that it does not end up in the shredder. Take catalogues around to each department and hand them out personally – this of course is the ideal situation but it may not prove possible to do in your organization. You do not have to produce the catalogues in a hardback format, some have been produced on disk and downloaded on to PCs through Lotus Notes.

One organization has taken the technology one step further and is developing catalogues on CD-ROM. The individual is able to click on the skill area they are interested in, then click on the preferred media; the package will then bring up a selection of suitable resources with a trailer of some of the recommended products. In complete contradiction to this the organization is also providing it in a hard copy format, perhaps for the benefit of the technophobes.

! Tip

There are organizations that will match resources to your needs and provide you with a catalogue at the same time, complete with detailed synopses.

Service questionnaires

Again as part of the evaluation, you need to keep an eye on how the staff view the centre. One way in which many organizations do this is by issuing a service questionnaire – this can be by way of a hard copy questionnaire to be completed, or can form part of an administration system. One idea may be to issue postcards to individuals, and again a competition element is one way of ensuring that it is completed. The sorts of questions that you may like to ask can be similar to your initial feedback ones, but you may also want to request information on any changes that the users may wish to be made within the centre. It may also be worth asking if the centre is meeting all of their development needs and if they feel that the marketing initiatives that you have conducted have had any effect on them at all.

Management of the centre

Unfortunately most organizations that decide to take the open learning centre route do not make adequate provision for its administration. There are very few learning centres that have been set up with a full-time administrator in place from the start. The reason for this is largely down to cost – the organization may have allocated £40,000 for resources but not be prepared to lay out a salary for the administrator, many saying that they will not do so until they can be sure that the centre is a success.

I can understand this hesitation, but how can an organization expect to run a successful centre if there is no one there to manage it? It is all very well and good to say that the training administrator can take responsibility for the centre along with their other duties, but all too often they are not given the time or the resources to dedicate to it and as a consequence the centre fails. If you open a staff shop people are not going to keep using it if there is never anyone there to serve them. We insist that if an organization is serious about a learning centre then a full-time administrator should be employed from the start. If this is done the centre is more likely to be a success, because the administrator is aware that if it fails then they could be out of a job! The other benefits of a full-time person dedicated to the centre is that they will operate it as a separate cost centre and will have the time to market it and ensure that everything is running smoothly. Some organizations have up to three full-time administrators solely responsible for the learning centre. This is not necessary at the outset, but obviously you hope to grow and you need to make allowances for these developments in future budgets.

The best person for the job

Many organizations have recruited from within to fill this position, usually from the training or HR departments. It is useful to have a familiar face looking after the centre, and even more valuable if they possess a training or HR background, as this is certain to add credibility to the centre. It also ensures that when individuals use the centre they are more likely to achieve valuable guidance and assistance in their search for the correct resource. Above all, whoever you decide to administer the centre must be trained thoroughly. The training should not just include advice on how to use CD-ROM, CD-I etc, but should ideally go one step further, and include training on the whole cycle of development, how people learn, the various learning styles, how different media can be used, and so on.

The credibility factor

The knowledge of the administrator and the support and assistance that they can provide to the users is imperative to the overall success of the centre. Making the right impression at the beginning is a vital ingredient, as people will base their under-standing of the centre's facilities on their personal experiences right from the start, and it is much harder (as we all know) to get new customers than it is to maintain existing ones.

As part of the training process, organize visits to other learning centres in order that your staff can discuss their concerns with other administrators; this will also help them to get guidance and indeed support from others in the same situation. Try to maintain contact and share ideas – if you have tried something that has proved successful then ring up and tell them; you are not in competition and if you do it they will respond in the same manner. Some organizations have set up learning centre networks, one of the most successful being instigated by Jim Plunkett of Atomic Weapons Establishment (AWE).

The role of the administrator

If the administrator is taken on purely to look after the centre, their responsibilities may include the following:

- ensuring that all users are put through an induction
- booking delegates into the centre
- logging out resources
- maintaining the appearance of the centre
- sending out reminder letters for overdue products
- making recommendation to individual users
- promoting the centre
- liaising with product suppliers
- providing technical support
- making recommendations for new product acquisition
- updating the catalogue
- providing reports on usage, etc.

When demand exceeds supply

In my experience one of the most common questions or concerns that people have when they are setting up an open learning centre is the demand versus supply situation. For example, what will happen if you have only two copies of a book, they are both on loan, and six people have requested it? Do you buy six more copies? Do you let them get frustrated because they will have to wait six weeks before they can have the book? What happens if you buy six more copies and no one ever uses the book again? The question of quantity is probably one of your biggest concerns at the moment, and justifiably so. Unfortunately I cannot tell you how many copies you should obtain, as I am not able to predict the future; the only advice I can give is based on my awareness of the success that other organizations have had when dealing with this situation.

The last thing anyone wants in their centre is a shelf full of resources that are collecting dust; this demonstrates a poor decision and a waste of resources, but sometimes it cannot be avoided. There will be new initiatives within the organization that may well instigate a surge of demand for a certain product, such as customer care, empowerment, self-managed teams, or a new IT initiative.

If purchasing several copies is physically not possible yet you still have the demand, consider offering individuals an alternative. It is largely with text-based material that you will encounter this situation, as they take a few days or weeks to read rather than half an hour to watch. If, for example, demand is due to a new customer service policy, suggest that the individual comes to the centre and watches a video, or uses the CD-ROM. They may not have considered these options, and you will be able to service a lot more customers, as it will only take half an hour to go through the package. If they are still insistent on reading a book, recommend an alternative title – most books on customer care tend to contain the same messages and principles so their needs will still be met.

93

If after all this they are still insistent then all you can do is remind the person who has the title when it must be returned and make them aware that there is now a substantial waiting list for it, or recommend that they ask their department to purchase it from their own budget. The latter should be your very last resort, as in future they may not see the point of coming to the learning centre if they feel that they will only end up having to pay for something out of their own or the departmental pocket. Video and other similar media are such costly items that it is more difficult to explain away wastage on products costing in excess of £800.

As a provider you will be required to meet the needs of your customers, so if you do get the demand there is no way around it – you will need to meet it. Every commercial organization creates waste, if they did not then factory outlet shops would be non-existent; so do not put yourself under any unnecessary pressure but be prepared for it. Allocate resources for this in your budget, and if you do find yourself with 50 copies of a now redundant title on your shelf put yourself into retail mentality. What do they do with last season's fashions? They do not leave them in the shop to collect dust, they have a sale! So do the same with your surplus! If it is politically possible, offer these titles for individuals to purchase, either out of their departmental budget or their personal one. Give them a good discount – offer them 20% off the rrp. When you sell something, put the money back into the resource centre's budget to purchase new product or to market the centre. If this is not feasible, instead of keeping an old product give it away – to individual staff, to a local library or school, or to a charitable organization. Look upon it as a part of the organization's commitment to supporting the local community.

There are other options available to you, such as 'revolving libraries' (discussed in Chapter 8), which enable you to have access to a large number of resources without having to purchase them first. In terms of video at the time of writing no such scheme exists, and the only option available to you is to join a hire plan, which means you pay upfront and can then take out a number of two-day hires throughout the year. This is not as cost effective, but things may change as the market moves increasingly towards resource-based learning.

How do you decide how many copies of each product to purchase during the early stages? This really is dependent on the individual organization but it also depends on the number of employees who will have access to the centre, and of course whether you will be loaning resources out. This is why the monitoring and evaluation process during the early stages is absolutely vital. The first three months should provide you with an adequate gauge of the areas and media that people are most interested in. But try to plan ahead, think about when you are likely to get a rush for certain products and try to ensure that you will be able to meet the demand. For example, make a note of the following dates:

- annual appraisals
- financial year end
- graduate intake
- professional examinations
- holidays
- induction programmes
- training courses.

As a general rule of thumb, do not be tempted to go overboard; it is always better to have a demand for product than it is to have a storeroom full of redundant material. Finding the balance is not easy – you cannot predict what the demand will be so it is best to aim somewhere between the potentially highest and lowest levels of usage. There will be certain issues within all organizations that you will need material to cover, and following is a list of the areas that my research has indicated are some of the most popular:

- customer care
- time management/personal organization
- stress management
- assertiveness
- IT skills
- keyboard skills
- coaching
- general management /supervisory skills
- delegation
- motivation
- teamwork
- leadership
- problem solving and creativity.

Another way of predicting usage is to look at the take-up of the training courses that the organization has in place – find out which are the most popular and when they are run. This will provide you with a good indicator of in which areas people feel the need for development. But remember that it is only an indication – do not take it for granted that just because people sign up for a course in assertiveness it means they will be flocking to the OLC for a copy of *Assertiveness at Work* by Ken and Kate Back. Some organizations always purchase two copies of everything for the centre, but as a rule these organizations have the budget which enables them to do this and may also have a customer base of over 15,000. If yours is nowhere near this then I would suggest that you initially buy one copy of each resource and through careful monitoring purchase a duplicate as and when necessary.

Complementing the training courses

One of the reasons for the failure of so many learning centres is a direct result of their isolation from the training and development function. The open learning centre should be seen as a complementary link to other forms of development processes, and to avoid any resistance you should be working hand in hand. The learning centre is not always the right or most effective solution to an individual's development needs, however it should be linked to and integrated with all kinds of other development activities.

For example, ensure that the materials in the centre are linked to appraisal and development plans. If an individual has identified a need it is up to you to determine the best course of action – this may be a training course, work-based activity or book to read. Ensure, too, that the training department is fully aware of the facilities that the learning centre provides. They have a captive audience – it may be that they recommend pre-course work that the individual is to conduct within the learning centre, or they may be aware of other needs that are identified following a course and be able to suggest that a visit to the learning centre would be of great value.

The learning environment

Many organizations that have set up learning centres have fallen short by ignoring the importance of the learning environment. We are all aware of the importance of this on a training course, so you cannot afford to overlook it when it comes to the learning centre. Ask yourself if you would feel comfortable sitting in the centre studying for a couple of hours.

- Are the chairs comfortable?
- Is the centre easy to find?
- Is there plenty of room for the resources?
- Is the lighting adequate?
- Is the temperature correct?
- Can you relax there?
- What is the noise level like?
- Is there a facility for obtaining refreshments?
- Is there room to expand?

All of these issues should be dealt with from the word go and should be taken very seriously. The provision of refreshments is an important one – if people can sit and relax with a cup of coffee while browsing through a development title they are more likely to return. Just think of the impact that the smell of freshly brewed coffee has on you!

Make sure that the centre looks appealing – if you take it seriously, so will your customers; if it looks shabby and untidy, people are less likely to take an interest in it. You do not have to spend a fortune on it, you can obtain all sorts of freebies. Ask producers to supply you with posters and dump bins for the centre, get as much as you can – after all, they want to receive some promotion as well and it is free advertising for them.

Credit Suisse have a fabulous way of getting people into their centre: it has the most impressive views over the Thames. Being located on the 17th floor has certainly proved an advantage, with many coming to the centre to admire the view. This is an excellent example of a learning centre that has taken as much time and thought over its location and environment as it has in the acquisition of the resources within it.

Some organizations have been lucky enough to have had a choice when it comes to the position of the centre, many deciding to place it next to the staff restaurant or on the ground floor next to reception. Others have used it as an exhibition piece, which can be seen from the outside of the building. This acts as a promotion tool to visitors, creating the idea that the organization has invested in development. There are clear advantages to this but there are some disadvantages, as it does not create a great impression if it is empty.

Alternatively, locate the centre next to the boardroom. It will certainly impress the senior managers if they see individuals taking time to develop themselves and, as you will see from the case studies, the level of management least likely to use the centre is in fact the senior level – if it is close to them you have a greater chance of getting them to use it!

! Tip

If you want to get some pictures to brighten up the centre, have a look through a Successorize catalogue for some that are powerful and inspirational. Or ask the local school or children's ward in a hospital to supply you with some of their drawings – organize a painting competition and invite the winner to the launch.

Most organizations are not this fortunate, with space being extremely limited, one organization used the room allocated for the learning centre as a hairdresser's. This I feel clearly demonstrates the management's opinion of developing its staff (ironically this particular organization does have the Investors in People Award). Ultimately, it may be necessary to make the most of the room that you have been given, but at least this gives you a chance to develop your resourcefulness. Some of the most successful centres have operated from the smallest of spaces, so it is true to say that a successful centre is very dependent on usage and what the users can get from it, rather than size (see the Sims case study on pages 165–7).

The use of music

Some centres have used music to create a calming and relaxing environment which is more conducive to the learning process, and this has often been an area of discussion within the more formal areas of training as well as in a self-development environment. Using music can aid the relaxation process, but of course you do need to think seriously about the kind of music that you will be playing – it may not be such a good idea to have Status Quo blaring out from the centre's doors. There are all sorts of music that you can obtain from a variety of stores that contain sounds which are particularly conducive to creating the kind of environment you wish to attain, but make sure that the music is not too loud, otherwise it will be detrimental to the learning process rather than beneficial.

Making the most of your cupboard

Just to reassure those organizations with a limited budget for their learning centre, I would like to discuss in this section just how you can get the most from a small or 'compact' learning centre. Several organizations with which we have come into contact simply do not have the resource to set up huge centres, and are given a budget with the proviso that they can expand if it proves successful. This can put you in a very difficult situation, especially if you find that demand more than outweighs supply. The negative consequence of this is that people may become disillusioned if they find that they are waiting six weeks for a book, or are unable to use the centre when they want to.

One way to approach this is to make the centre available to individual departments at a particular time, almost as a pilot, then as the board see that the trial is successful you can push for more space and resources. Another solution is not to have people use the centre but for it to act more as a distance library; you can easily fool people as to the size of the centre if they never actually see it. Having some sort of facility far outweighs not having one at all.

If you are in a situation where you are very short of budget, for example if your organization is a charity, you can improvise and still make the most of your limited resource if you know how. One such organization that really did have to beat the budget barrier was Scope (formerly known as the Spastics Society). Scope had a budget of £2,000 to set up a learning resource facility for their staff – a pretty hard task, if not an impossible one. But working to such a tight budget often means that the resources you have will definitely be the right ones for the staff using them.

In assessing suitable resources the choice of media is often limited. With most CD-ROM and CD-I packages within the £1000 region we had to look at alternatives, and being aware that different learning styles needed to be addressed meant that our main option was text based. However, there are many extremely useful books around costing in the region of £7; for example, look at the *Training Extras* series from the IPD, the *Better Management Skills* series from Kogan Page (with over 50 titles and growing), *Successful in a Week* series and the *Management Pocketbooks* from Melrose.

Most people prefer something light to read, something that they can digest in small, bite-sized chunks. Too many business books contain far too much jargon for the average person – they may seem fine to us but then we are used to many of the terms that are used. People will read short, succinct books which contain handy tips and hints that they can also use as a reference guide.

In addition to books there are a lot of computer-based packages around that have come down in price due to competition from CD-ROMs, etc. These can be excellent tools that provide a good degree of interaction. Audio is another useful mechanism which again is very inexpensive, and never forget that not all training videos cost £900 – there are some excellent ones around for as little as £49.

If you are a charitable organization, do not forget that many producers and publishers have a standard discount set up for you, for example Training Direct offers a 20 per cent discount to all charities. Another way of getting material is to ask for freebies, and there are all kinds of ways in which you can obtain free material if you don't mind asking, as I found out when working for Scope. Many organizations are more than happy to offload any excess material that they hold in return for a little good PR. Scope received hundreds of books from Midland Bank's learning facility LEAP, simply because we asked.

We also found that it is possible to acquire free or heavily discounted books from some of the mainstream publishers, who often have a number of books which cannot be sold to the public for various reasons. These books simply sit in storage or are destroyed, and some publishers are often more than happy to supply you with a collection of these. Remember if you do not ask you do not get!

Ask the producers and publishers of resources for promotional material, such as posters. It is often the physical appearance of the OLC that your organization may object to funding due to political issues, so some free posters could be just the thing you need to brighten up your centre.

Checklist

☐ Ask for free material from publishers and producers.
☐ Ask for promotional material.

Support

This is a critical area as far as the success of the learning centre is concerned. It is all well and good encouraging individuals to develop themselves, but we cannot expect them to be completely autonomous. What support should you provide and who should be responsible for it? As every organization is different, you may find that the needs of the users are also unique.

Support is imperative, as without it the users could become disheartened and demotivated. It may not necessarily be the training department that provides this support – you could make it the responsibility of the line manager, or you might want to consider asking a mix of managers, identified as having a particular skill in staff development and/or coaching, to become learner supporters. Their responsibility would be to ensure that the needs of the individuals are being met

Learning advisers

Many organizations have taken the opportunity to recruit, either externally or from within, the support of a 'learning adviser'. This person's responsibility is to assist the line managers with their own development and the development of their staff. They act in a similar manner to area trainers or coaches who are responsible to the training or HR department, and the role can either be full or part time, depending upon the size of the organization.

The learning adviser's main task is to support the department, and to support the managers – they do not move away from the self-development process as they are not recruited to tell but to support and to provide guidance. You cannot expect a manager to suddenly be able to take the initiative to develop themselves without any support whatsoever – they do need help and advice. Often it is not possible to obtain this kind of assistance from the training department, the managers need someone to be at hand and a learning adviser can be the perfect solution. If you decide that recruiting these advisers is the right solution they will of course need to be trained.

If learning advisers have not been taken from the training department they will need to be aware of the way in which people learn and the opportunities that are available to them in terms of development. They can therefore prove to be excellent advocates of the learning centre. This may not be the answer to a training need on every occasion, but having an awareness of what the learning centre contains will enable them to sell the concept when appropriate.

Setting up multiple sites

It may be that your organization has decided that more than one centre is required in order to provide an effective service to your customers. This is often the case in the retail sector, where the majority of users are based in branches across the country. Many organizations have gone down this route, providing mini-learning centres in a number of different locations.

Of course, setting up numerous centres at one time is much more time consuming that setting up one, and first of all you need to ensure that you really do need the number of locations that you have outlined. There are a number of factors that need to be taken into consideration when setting up a series of centres.

First, you will have to get support from each of the branch offices. It can create enormous problems if you do not involve them, and simply tell them that in three months' time they will have an open learning centre. Second, it is a good idea to get branch managers on your side by involving them as much as possible in the setting-up stage. And third, remember that you do not have to do everything centrally; the managers will be more aware of the materials that will be of value to their staff than you are. Taking their advice on board will save you making some expensive mistakes (which you will be reminded of at every opportunity).

Selecting resources

Some organizations with multiple centres have simply decided on core materials, and the same products are then purchased for each site. If you feel that the needs of everyone in the organization are identical then this may well be the solution; however, it may have been indicated that there are different needs in certain areas and you may need to adjust the resources that you acquire as a result. It is a good idea to have a variety of resources within the centres, as you will be able to rotate them across the board. This is a very cost-effective way of having a larger amount of resources; it also means that your users will think that you are continually updating the centre with new resources, when in fact all you are doing is swapping them with other centres.

Once you have acquired the resources then you need to ensure that, as with one site, they are catalogued and logged. This information should then be disseminated to the other resource centre administrators in order that they can see exactly what is available in all of the centres, which will enable you to provide your customers with a more efficient service. For example, if the book they request is not available within your centre then you will be able to check its availability at the other sites. This is where a good administration software system would prove invaluable.

Promoting the centres

This can be done in exactly the same way as a single centre; however, you may want to delegate this to the individual branch managers, who may have different methods of communicating information internally, and who may also feel that the way the message is communicated should be done in their own particular style. If this is the case, it is not worth fighting for a common identity – you will only end up with resentful branch managers, and it is absolutely vital at this stage that they be on your side.

If you decide that you want a name and logo for the centre then it is a good idea to ensure that there is uniformity. This will not only be much cheaper when it comes to creating catalogues and promotional material, but will also provide a common identity for resource centres within the organization. Another point worth considering is whether each of the learning centres will physically operate in the same manner, ie will they be open the same length of time? Will the media be the same? These are areas that you need to give some thought to well in advance of setting up the centres.

The launch

The launch process for multiple sites can be as indicated for a single one (see Chapter 11). It is not, however, always the best idea to have the launch dates too close together or, indeed, too far apart. Many organizations have conducted a common launch for all of the centres while others have left it up to the individual sites. If you do decide on the latter option it is still a good idea to provide them with some guidance, this may be in the form of a pack which outlines various formats of launch they may wish to conduct.

Marketing multi-site learning centres

It may be that you choose a central function for the marketing of all of the centres, or it may be that you decide to make it the responsibility of each of the centre managers. There are advantages and disadvantages to each of these. If it is the responsibility of each independent centre the manager is likely to take more responsibility for it; however, they may need some guidance and support, and this is where the importance of internal communication and support kicks in.

Ensure that the managers are prepared to exchange ideas, sharing what has worked or not worked for their own particular centre. It may also be suggested that they have learning centre forums; these could be held on a monthly or quarterly basis, during which people are encouraged to share their ideas and provide each other with support. It may be that you choose a combination of central, and more local, marketing activity. As long as it proves effective it does not really matter which route you choose, but it is best to ensure that a common message is portrayed to the users and that there is a degree of continuity.

International open learning centres

If your organization is one which has offices world-wide, you may wish to make the facility that you have available within the UK to employees across the globe. There are several different ways of achieving this. You can send materials out to them on a loan basis, as you would with branches in the UK, but this is of course much more difficult to control, and you need to be aware of the licensing agreements with your resources. Do not forget to take into consideration the differences in technology and equipment.

If you would rather that the individual branches have their own centres, and you require them to use the same materials as you hold within the UK, check the availability of independent centres and resource suppliers in the relevant countries. Many of the higher profile organizations will have outlets in most countries, and there are independent suppliers that will be able to advise your branches on the best resources to suit their needs.

Marketing your centre

Once you have had the launch and everyone is aware of the learning centre, it is very tempting to sit back and think that the hardest part is over, and that all you need to do now is wait for the masses to come knocking on the door to book themselves in. If you do this the centre will probably be fine for a few months but then the phone will get quieter and so will the centre; with the pressures of work and home the launch of the centre, and indeed self-development, will be nothing but a distant memory for most people – except of course for you.

Do not be tempted to think like this. Look upon the centre in the same way that you would look upon a new restaurant opening in your home town. The restaurant is unique, the food is great, you go to investigate the first week of opening because you see it advertised, and you promise yourself that you will go back. A few months later you have forgotten what the restaurant was called, you've never seen it advertised, and probably it has closed down. This is exactly what will hapen to your OLC. Just because you are aware that it is still there do not assume that everyone else will be. They need reminding, so once the launch is over start preparing your marketing plan – if you have not done so already.

It is usual to have a huge amount of interest during the first three months, as people are intrigued and feel quite motivated, but the novelty soon wears off, and this is when they need to be attacked by a well thought-out marketing programme. This next section will look at ways in which you can maintain a high level of usage within your OLC, both soon after it has opened and over the long term. These are simply a collection of ideas that have been tried and tested by some organizations, it is not a definitive list, because what works for one organization may not work for yours.

As I mentioned previously, you are not restricted to having one launch for the centre – a launch can be something that takes place every year. Some organizations have in fact relaunched their centre, but remember not to start marketing the centre when the usage factor is dropping – ensure that you make it a continuous affair.

The relaunch

A relaunch can be an event which is very similar in format to your initial launch, but this does not mean that you need to repeat everything that you did initially. You do not need to recut the ribbon, for example, but many of the activities you did first time around can remain the same. The National Audit Office recently held a very successful event to rekindle interest in their centre – the event took place at their head office in London, with producers and publishers invited to attend to exhibit their wares. It was by no means a sales event, organizations were chosen that could add value to the whole concept of self-development across a broad range.

Each organization took along samples of their product, from CD-ROM to text-based material, and Peter Honey attended to discuss self-development with individuals who required advice. The event allowed individuals to see exactly what materials they could have access to and they were invited to jot down any materials that they saw that they would like to see included within the OLC. The occasion stimulated interest in self-development as well as acting as a catalyst which enabled the training team to see exactly what needs the individuals had.

In terms of cost, most of the producers and publishers attended free of charge, seeing it as invaluable opportunity to market their services. An event of this nature of course takes time to plan, but the results more than reward the time and effort that you need to put in.

Another idea is to hold regular events that cover particular issues. For example, you could hold a self-development fair, where you invite an independent supplier to bring along a range of resources that cover 'personal development', or if you have competencies in place you might like to hold events which look at some of these, and have materials that will help people achieve them.

Zeneca in Manchester has been holding events of this nature for the past two years, and has found them to be extremely successful. They hold the event over two or three days and produce a catalogue which is mailed in advance to all employees, enabling them to decide on the materials that they would like to come and see. During the fair individuals are encouraged to order materials from the selection – they can buy for themselves or for their department – or resources that they would like to be held centrally in the OLC.

This kind of event enables individuals to see the resources, and enables you to keep up to date with all the new materials that have emerged. But perhaps most importantly it increases people's awareness of the facility that you can provide – many probably do not realize that you have CD-ROM in the centre, and many may not be aware of the sheer volume of books that you hold. It also makes them feel involved in the centre; by allowing them to choose the resources for the centre you are encouraging them to take responsibility not only for their own development but for that of others, too (which is surely what a learning organization is all about).

When thinking about holding an event try to link it to initiatives that are happening within the organization – keep your eyes and ears open. If you hear that there is going to be a new customer service policy, think about holding an event around that issue. Market the materials that you have on customer service, send out flyers, put up posters, e-mail people – whatever it takes. Use all forms of communication to make the most of the opportunity. You could even get a guest speaker along who is known as a guru on customer service. If you do not have the space to hold it in the learning centre, don't worry, just make sure that you take plenty of materials around that subject area in the room where it will be held.

You can try the same process whenever a new software package is introduced; inform people about the range of self-development tools that are contained within the learning centre. Some organizations even have weekly lunchtime surgeries where people can go and get advice on particular IT problems they are encountering with the new or existing software.

Another angle on this is to market the vulnerable. I do not mean the weak and unstable, I mean targeting the new recruits, particularly graduates, school-leavers and temporary staff. They may well have been on an IT training course but they may want to speed up their skills with some extra tuition; or they might have felt a little embarrassed on the course and could benefit from spending some time improving or brushing up on some areas at their own pace and in their own time.

Other events to consider involve targeting particular people rather than specific issues. I have already mentioned graduates, but think about the following categories too.

Women

Look at the mix of employees within the organization. Do you have a database of personnel records that you can access to conduct mailshots, for example and, if you do, what categories are they in?

All marketing activities are conducted to targeted groups and records kept in order to easily recognize particular sectors at which to aim. Advertisers direct their advertisements at the majority of viewers they wish to target for a particular product. They look at generalizations and common traits. For example, if an organization wishes to advertise a new children's toy it will put the advert on TV at around 4pm or on a Saturday morning, when it knows that a large proportion of the target audience will be watching. My point is that you too, need to match your product to individual needs, make it specific to the individual.

We all want something that we feel has been specifically designed to meet our particular requirements, and you are in the best position to make this seem the case. For example, identify what most women's training or development needs are in business today. Most appear to demand material that covers personal development, but in particular assertiveness, self-esteem, how to juggle work and home, excelling in business, breaking the glass ceiling etc. Try holding events which allow the women in your organization the opportunity to view these materials or invite a guest speaker along – contact the local business club to find out the name of a particularly successful business woman in the area and whether she would be prepared to come along and give a lunchtime seminar.

Or you could make it health related. With increasing concern over issues such as breast cancer and cervical cancer, you could invite someone along to discuss these issues. It may be worth stocking a video in the centre on self-examination, and this could also be included for the male counterparts too, as testicular cancer is just as much an issue in today's society as breast cancer is.

You could also look at other health-related events, such as general good nutritional advice or stress management. I am not suggesting that the learning centre become a clinic by any means, but it is all in the name of changing the culture. People should see the centre as a service, and if they become used to using material for self-development in these areas it will soon become habitual and they will think of the centre when looking at other learning needs.

Other ideas include events around physical self-presentation. One of the best-selling books for learning centres in the non-vocational areas has been *Presenting Yourself*, published by Piatkus. You could contact The Federation of Image Consultants (0956 701018) and invite a local consultant to come along to the centre to give a presentation on their work, which includes advising clients on their best clothing colours and shapes. This need not be an expensive option, especially if you allow the consultant to mention follow-up courses or private consultations. You can, of course, invite male employees to this event, but it might be more beneficial to run separate sessions. Consider, too, including women returning to the workplace. It is sometimes very difficult to make the transition, as not only will individuals have changed during their absence but so, too, will the organization.

Older employees

Another group on your target hit list should be those who you know are nearing retirement age. Send them an invitation to attend an event that will provide them with some useful advice on what to do when they retire, and again get someone along to help, with advice on life after work. The centre could also hold some publications on retirement, writing a will, pensions etc. There is quite a lot of useful material out there that looks specifically at these areas, so make sure that you make potential users aware of it.

Younger employees

Based on research, the average age of a person using a learning centre is between 26 and 40 years old; this means that you really do need to target the younger employee quite heavily. It is very difficult to persuade someone who is only 17 and in their first job that even though they have just come out of school, they should be prepared to go back to it.

Many of the barriers that you will face will be a result of the misconceptions people have about self-development and the materials that are provided, and this is why it is important that these be eliminated from the mind of the school-leaver. You need to make the centre part of their culture as soon as possible, and you need to dispel any prejudices that they may have.

How do you do this? Well, think about the issues that are of interest to younger people, such as travel. If all they are thinking about is their 24 days holiday, you could hold events on travel destinations. Ask a travel organization if they can arrange for someone to come and talk about a particular country that you feel may be of interest, and tie this in with the particular language. Include time for them to have a look at the materials that you have in the centre.

These workshops prove particularly useful at Easter time, when the advent of warmer weather and longer days sets people thinking about their holiday destinations, or follow the advertisers' example and hold them after Christmas. This can be especially beneficial to the organization as well as to the individual, as morale is particularly low at this time of year, following all the hype of Christmas and new year, coupled with shorter days and cold weather.

You could also invite someone along to give advice on managing their personal finances, as many of these individuals will not have received a salary before; some may not even have a bank account, so personal budgeting is completely alien to them, but advice on this area may be more than welcome. Again do not do all the work yourself – invite a speaker from a local bank or insurance company and get them to have a look at some of the material that you have on the subject.

I have mentioned only a few of the groups that you could target – it is up to you to think about your organization and who the target groups are within it. The main idea is to think about individual's needs; try not to look at the audience as the same set of customers, because they are not, and each one will have a very different shopping list.

Checklist

☐ Think of four groups, not already mentioned, that you could target

☐ Think about specific events that you could hold for each group.

Activity

Name of group

1 .... Event

2 .... Event

3 .... Event

4 .... Event

The family

Some centres have made the centre available not just for employees, but have gone one step further and allowed their families access. This has a great effect on usage figures but can be difficult to control, so if you do decide to take this route then you will need to consider how you will administer it. Will you only allow direct family, ie spouses and children? When will they have access? The last thing you want is to have the centre fully booked to family, resulting in direct employees having to wait up to two weeks to gain access. It may be worth allowing families access during the quieter periods only. It is up to you to decide but, whatever you decide, you need to make a decision at the beginning rather than change the rules half way through.

Meetings

If your centre can accommodate it, then make it available for hire. Obviously you cannot make it available all the time, but you could do so once a month, or when you know occupancy is low. Advertise this facility on a noticeboard or put it in the brochure which contains the opening times of the centre. Make people aware that if they do hire the centre they are more than welcome to use all of the facilities contained within it.

If the usage factor of the centre is exceptionally high I would not advise doing this as you will only irritate your current customers by denying them access. However, you may feel that Monday mornings are particularly quiet and that it would be well worth putting the room to good use for at this time. One audience who would be more than worth enticing along to the centre by this method would be the senior managers, although unfortunately it is the senior managers who are least likely to run out of meeting-room space.

Technology days

I have already mentioned the popularity of using new software initiatives as a mechanism to draw people into the centre, but what about mere technology? Many people (particularly those of a more mature age), suffer from technophobia, and technology days can provide them with an opportunity to get to grips with concepts such as e-mail and the Internet. One organization had an exceptional response to an event entitled 'Teach me Technology Today', the idea being to give people a basic awareness of multimedia and the Internet. Most people claimed they knew about it, but when they were asked what they thought 'multimedia' meant, there were some very interesting responses.

Most people of a certain age are not uninterested in new technology, but feel completely daunted by it. They cannot ask their children, and feel uncomfortable asking a subordinate, preferring either to remain ignorant or simply to muddle through, almost as if there is an enormous amount of shame to be attached to the fact that they do not know how to surf the Net.

The learning centre is the ideal forum for people like this to familiarize themselves with such technology, as they are able to learn in a non-threatening environment, exposing their ignorance quite openly. It proves a safe mechanism for guiding senior managers too, who certainly do not wish others to be aware of their shortcomings. An event of this nature can take several formats: a formal all-day course, or an open day where people are made welcome to attend the centre to use some of your resources to increase their knowledge of how such technology can best be utilized.

Induction

Ensuring that an introduction to the learning centre is part of the induction process is of paramount importance. Just as new recruits are shown the health and safety regulations, so they should be shown the mechanism by which they can develop themselves. There will be a lot to absorb on joining the company, and it may well be that some of this information is contained within the learning centre. Some learning centres have put an induction package on to CD-ROM, so that individuals can work their way around the different departments without leaving their seats. The package can contain information on company history, who's who, holiday allowances, pay systems etc. Some organizations have even made this available at reception, in order that visitors can find out more information about the company that they are visiting. Beats reading a copy of *Mortgage Weekly*!

Language learning

We discussed the benefits of having non-vocational material within the centre and how it can act as an effective way of getting people into the centre in Chapter 9, but you should not just purchase these resources solely for this purpose. If you have these materials then take full advantage of them. It may be that the organization requests these resources as a business need, and advocates quite strongly the acquisition of a second language.

Whatever the reason, if you do have language resources within the centre, consider starting formal language learning sessions. Organize evenings or lunch hours where people can join a 'language learning circle', which will act as a motivational tool to get people to use the centre on a more regular basis. Promote the fact that every Tuesday evening or Thursday lunchtime (or whenever) those who wish to learn or improve upon a second language can come in to the centre to use the facilities that you have.

Many people are embarrassed when attending language classes, so if they feel that they can learn in a non-threatening environment they are more likely to attend. The other advantage is that they can leave when they want without disturbing anyone, and can learn at their own pace. Of course, they can come in at any time to use the language facilities, but by dedicating a couple of hours a week you will find that people will make more of an effort to attend. It will become habitual, they will find support and comfort from others who are learning a language, and will be able to discuss their own particular needs with others in a similar situation.

One thing you must bear in mind when allocating special times to specific events is that you do not want to push your existing customers out. Be careful. Ensure that you choose a time when the centre is rarely used, and if someone does want to use the centre during this time do not discourage them from doing so, but make certain that they are aware of what is happening within the centre.

There are some great language resources on the market, and they are relatively inexpensive; for example Libra has just brought out a range of CD-ROM packages for under £100 per course (see Appendix VI for further details).

Revision facilities

Another way of increasing usage within the centre is to make an area available for those who are studying for professional qualifications (which is another reason why it is a good idea to have the main core of textbooks within the centre). Do bear in mind that you will need to have a substantial amount of space, as they do tend to come in large, A3 formats, and in several volumes – if you have ever seen the textbooks for the ACCA then you will know exactly what I mean.

You also need to be careful here that demand does not exceed supply, as you could end up with a large portion of your budget allocated to these, leaving you with little room and little money for anything else. I would suggest that you keep only one copy of each for reference purposes, and allow them to be taken out only in exceptional circumstances.

If you do decide to include these materials, make adequate provision in your budget for updates, because once you have these resources in place people will expect you to keep them up to date. Ensure that those concerned are aware that the resources are there for their use, and suggest that individuals may use the centre for revision purposes if need be. It may be an idea to block out time for these individuals, but again make sure that this is at a time when the centre is not in great demand. Providing this facility does of course depend on the opening hours of the centre – if you are only open during business hours it may not be possible, as the centre should be in full use.

Roadshows

Some organizations have looked at alternative ways of promoting their centres, and one which has proved very successful has been the 'roadshow'. A roadshow suggests that the service you provide is taken to various sites in order that those who cannot come to you are able to see the extent of your service for themselves. This is ideal if your learning centre services several sites, or where most people have a catalogue of resources from which they can hire or borrow material but where they cannot physically get to the centre. I feel this is relevant to most organizations where, nine times out of ten, there is initially only one OLC, based at head office, but which is required to serve a number of other sites and/or branches. If this is the case for you (as it is with Norwich Union), you may wish to consider the roadshow option. What does it involve?

It is up to you to decide on the scale of the roadshows, but generally it entails organizing a series of events throughout the different sites where you take along a good cross-section of the resources contained within your centre. This should include a full range of media; for example, if you have CD-ROM or CD-I, you should most definitely take this with you, even though they may not have the facility to use these resources at a particular site. Your objective is to make people aware of the media available and again to try to change the culture. It may even be that on seeing these resources they are in a stronger position to push for a learning centre of their own. Include plenty of text-based material, but do some research first, making sure that you find out what the particular needs of that branch are – they will probably be different to those of HQ. There may even be specific initiatives in place, so think about taking material that links to these.

Treat roadshows as a series of mini-launches. Your objective is to get as many people interested in open learning as possible, and you may also have to overcome some resistance. They may feel a little resentful towards you, asking why head office should have the OLC and not themselves, so be prepared for this kind of reaction. Ensure that you plan the roadshows well in advance and check with each site to make certain that the day that you are proposing to come does not conflict with anything. You will need to give people plenty of notice, design a flyer with the relevant dates and times, and incorporate a competition element to gain extra interest. You could even have a national open learning competition where branches compete against one another, or you could have a league which determines which branch is using the centre most, and give a quarterly prize to the winner.

! Tip

The roadshow does not have to take place on site – think about using external venues, such as a local hotel.

Remember that you should also provide some kind of facility whereby people can request resources, as it may prove the ideal opportunity for them to ask for certain materials. You cannot purchase everything that people request, but try to purchase some. These events act as a great mechanism through which to obtain feedback about the service that you are providing, and will certainly help you in the evaluation process of the centre.

Design a questionnaire – ask them if they are really pleased with the service that you are providing and find out why if they are not. It is also a good opportunity for you to discuss ways in which development material can help individual needs, so talk to people to find out what their needs are and recommend resources that you think will help them.

A roadshow is by no means an easy event to coordinate and it can become very exhausting, particularly if you have 20 branches to get around, but it has proved to be a very successful and rewarding mechanism for getting people interested in the OLC. Be warned that planning is crucial, and make certain that the dates are not too close together, otherwise you will soon find yourself becoming tired, irritable and stale. You will probably be asked the same questions 20 or 30 times, and you will be continually unpacking and repacking, which is not one of the most pleasant tasks in the world.

If you have the resources at hand it is best to split the roadshows between two people. This ensures that a fresh approach is taken each time, and will also mean that the centre back at HQ does not become neglected. If you can ask one of the training team to be responsible, it will act as a good bonding mechanism and provide you with a well-deserved break!

Even if all the staff within your organization are based at head office a roadshow is not necessarily out of the question; the name does imply taking the show on the road, but you could equally take the show to other departments in the building.

Never assume that just because you mailed everyone 16 times this year about the OLC that they will know about its existence. Think about how much mail you bin without even opening the envelope – internal mail is no different. Just to prove this, one organization (Thames Valley Police) hand-delivered a large number of catalogues about their OLC; when they did their analysis they found that only 60 per cent said that they had received one! The point is that it can be harder to get those who have direct access to use the centre than those who have to make a concerted effort – just like people who live in Windsor who have never visited the castle, when people come to see it from the other side of the world!

Try holding departmental days, where you take a mini-learning centre to departments for a certain period of time. Make someone responsible for its usage so that they can take responsibility for providing you with feedback. If possible, take a multimedia player which can act as a great incentive as it will arouse people's curiosity. If you have identified 'learning champions' then give them the responsibility for the mini-learning centre.

Make sure that you get permission first from the department head, as they may not be too pleased if people keep disappearing from their work stations to have a play with the various machines. If for whatever reason even a localized roadshow of this nature is beyond reach, go back to basics and do as Mortgage Express have been doing successfully for years – get a tea trolley and wheel the resources around to the departments. This might sound absurd, but if you think back to the last time you were in hospital you will remember quite vividly the revolving library. It is a very cost-effective way of promoting the centre and may well be the best solution. Your objective is to help people develop, it does not really matter what the mechanism is to encourage it – and it is often the more obscure ideas that really work.

The learning bus

Instead of having roadshows, try a mobile unit a little along the lines of a play bus which you can drive around the various branches. This is a great alternative to having additional centres and is an excellent way of gaining enthusiasm in self-development. It need not be a permanent fixture, but something that you could use twice a year just for promotional activity. You do not need a double-decker bus (and this is anyway not always feasible or practical), but a van equipped with resources like those used by mobile libraries is ideal. You need only put a selection of resources in it, and make sure that employees are aware of the dates and times when you will be passing through.

Newsletters

Why do we produce newsletters? To keep people informed of the latest developments, to increase a sense of belonging, to make people aware of the organization's and individual's achievements. I would agree that it is for all of these reasons, and suggest you produce a newsletter for the learning centre. It does not have to be a glossy affair, but it should look professionally presented.

Keeping people up to date with the progress of the learning centre serves a dual purpose: it can act as a marketing tool, a reminder to people that the learning centre is still there; and it can provide senior management with the reassurance that their money has been well spent and that the centre is providing a very valuable service to individuals as well as to the organization. How often you produce it is entirely up to you, and is of course dependent on the amount of time that you have available to produce it. A quarterly newsletter is ideal, but if this is not possible an annual one can be just as effective, and any form of communication on your part is better than none at all.

What it should contain

Think about the content of the organization's newsletter – do you read it? And if you do, why? Think about the reason behind producing a newsletter – are you using it as a sales tool or merely to inform? The best and most effective newsletters I have come across have been an amalgamation of the two. They have included information about the centre, reminding people of the facility and its opening hours etc, publicity on new products the centre has acquired, details of any events/roadshows that will be taking place, and information relevant to individuals. For example, if you have decided to run competitions and have allocated points to usage then you can announce the results in the newsletter – it will provide individuals with a sense of gratification when they see that they are at the top of the scale by accumulating 700 points at the learning centre. Any sense of achievement should be formally recognized, which may well act as an incentive to get others to use the centre more (which is of course your objective) and, if you link this to any promotions that have been made, it will illustrate the importance of the learning centre significantly.

To ensure that people read the newsletters instead of putting them straight through the shredder, try including a competition element. Choose questions that will force people to visit the learning centre, for example, 'Which character from *Eastenders* stars in a film on motivation?'

Activity

Jot down all the areas that you will cover in the newsletter

....

....

....

....

....

Your competition question

....

125

New products

One way in which you can promote new products within the learning centre is by way of the newsletter, but why wait? As soon as you have something new, tell people about it.

It does not matter how much new product you have – it may only be two new books, but you should promote them. Producing posters is a great way to make people aware of the product. Try getting these from the producer or publisher first, as often they will have a stock of promotional materials that they can let you have free of charge. If this is not the case, an alternative way to get free promotional material, especially for books, is to ask for a book jacket; publishers usually print these for all new titles in order that they can promote them at trade fairs etc. Ask them to provide you with a few for your own publicity.

As a last resort you can develop something internally, and once you have developed it all you need to do is stick copies up. Put them anywhere you can – lifts, canteens, staff shops, every department. It is always better to overstate than understate, but whatever you do make sure that you get permission first, the board may not take too kindly to your billboard activities, so do check.

Breakfast launches

If you have the budget you could even go one step further and organize a special event – either a breakfast or lunchtime seminar – and invite the author of the new title to come and talk about his or her book. You will need to contact the publisher first to organize this, and it is highly unlikely that they will do this for free, but if you can get the budget it is certainly worth doing, senior managers in particular will love it – especially if the person is of the right 'breeding'. I am not suggesting that you ask Tom

Peters to pop in for a filtered coffee and a Danish pastry, but there are other established 'gurus' who may be within your price range.

Linking up with this, when you do purchase new material try to keep an eye out for the latest Charles Handy, or Tom Peters title, and as soon as you have it make sure that the senior managers are aware – they too should be staying abreast of the latest strategic business initiatives, so see it as your role to provide them with the materials. After a while you may find the senior managers asking you advice on material suitable for them – a great honour!

It is important to keep the senior management content; if they see that the centre is providing them with a good service they are more likely to provide you with funding for the marketing events that have been discussed.

E-mail is another great medium by which you can communicate with people. You can market all sorts of your services through this – whether a new product or an event. Remember to keep your message short and snappy, people are receiving increasing amounts of information and can be selective about what they read.

Checklist

☐ Mail new products.
☐ Keep senior managers updated.

The learning club – membership, social events etc

One way to stimulate usage of the centre is to look upon the centre as a sort of club, a bit like a gym or social club – the route to self-development *is* very similar to that of keeping fit: you become aware that you have a need to improve your health (identified either by yourself or your GP), you know what you should be doing to improve it, but is not in your nature to do so. Our habits are formed at an early stage, and our learning habits are much like our eating ones. We get accustomed to eating certain kinds of food because we have always done so; we usually have three meals a day and we usually have the same things, but anyone who has ever had to change their dietary pattern for whatever reason knows how difficult it can be.

It is now medically proven that in order to lose weight permanently we must change the way in which we eat for the rest of our lives. Crash dieting is ineffective and often harmful – it is our eating habits that we need to change for ever. In order to change our habits we are given food plans or diet sheets, a bit like a development plan, so we know what we can and cannot eat. We have been given a path, with timescales, targets and objectives, and if we do attend a gym or slimming club we are monitored on a regular basis so that we can see the progress that we have made. But you know how difficult is it to motivate yourself to go to the gym before or after work – you know that you'll enjoy it once you get there, but you just never seem to be able to get there. This is very much like the thought processes we have when it comes to our own development: we know we need to do it, and we really deep down want to, but we just cannot seem to find the discipline or motivation to get there. However, if we start to go every Wednesday it soon becomes a habit, and we think of doing nothing else; the time is already allocated, and it is even easier when you go with a colleague, because you can be sure that if you don't feel like going they will convince you otherwise.

Going to the learning centre is not so very different, which is why people should be encouraged to go in groups. Learning sets are becoming more and more popular as people realize the real benefits of group learning for support and feedback. Apart from the health aspect of the gym, it may be becoming more popular because people like to be part of something, whether it is a religion, lifestyle or health club.

Make the most of this aspect of human nature by making your centre into a club. Provide people with membership cards and joining packs. Every gym has an induction process, every new member must undergo at least an hour's worth of training in order to become familiar with how to use the machines safely and effectively. The process should be the same within the OLC – new users should be shown how to use all the equipment. Inductions can be held in groups and conducted three times a day or so. Ask what the individual's objectives are in using the centre, and write their objectives down.

! Tip

Buy some postcards and get new members to state their short-term objective in using the centre. Put their address on the card and post it to them as a reminder in a couple of weeks' time.

Put charts up on the wall – you do not have to state individual's objectives for all to see, but you can recognize those who have achieved them.

You could try putting up notices on each of the machines to stimulate a competitive element, for example by offering a prize to those who obtain a certain amount of usage within a given period of time. A sticker attached to the multimedia station could say '½ hour = 10 points', and you could give prizes for those who achieve an excess of 100 points.

Some organizations have done something similar but offer air miles, so each time a member completes a CD-ROM course they gain a certain number of air miles that can be cashed in at any time. Others offer rewards when individuals get to certain stages – a common feature of many health clubs to get people to come back. It may seem superficial, but stating that they'll get a free T-shirt when they have spent 12 hours of study in the learning centre really does work.

Research conducted by Air Miles found that 62 per cent of rewards given within organizations were largely cash based, in the form of a bonus or profit share, but the research also showed that this is not the most effective way of motivating staff, as it simply pre-empted the 'Why is it only £X instead of £Y?' If we are to believe as, Maslow and Hertzberg suggest, that we should find other means of rewarding people based on their needs, surely we should be advocating that principle within the learning centre.

The use of incentives is certainly not a new one, and some organizations offer training courses as a reward for good performance. This may motivate some people but I must admit that I would not see it as being of personal benefit to me, as it is still work related. Many people would view this as the organization simply wanting to make them more effective employees for the organization's benefit, not the individual's.

What makes you buy one brand of crisps instead of another? You may have several reasons – taste, packaging, availability, cost – but what if you were offered a free video player if you collected 300 tokens from a particular brand? Tobacco companies have been using this method to encourage repeat sales for years, and it has proved to work – so why not try it in the OLC? If you decide that you do want to create a club-like environment, go one step further and organize social events for the users too.

Give the club a name and organize events that are not necessarily linked to development at all; you could start a bowling team, organize theatre trips, holidays, social evenings out etc. If it takes off, others in the organization may want to join the centre purely to benefit from the social side – it does not matter what their reasons are for joining initially, what counts is that they are using the facility.

Learning incentives

I discussed the potential problems that you will encounter when trying to get people into the centre in Chapter 2, and put forward some suggestions there on how to avoid them. We have also looked at the centre from a selling side, but what about the reward aspect? The competition element is clearly something which should prove beneficial to your employees and organization, but there is also the possibility of offering some kind of pay-related incentive linked to usage. This idea is by no means a revolutionary one, as organizations have been offering incentives of this nature for years, particularly to reward sales staff for their efforts; but some organizations have taken this idea a step further and have used the same principle to reward those who have excelled in their own development.

One organization within the financial services sector offers a substantial remuneration to those employees who achieve their target level of competence, and as they have made the training department into a support unit employees can only achieve this through self-development mechanisms.

I am not suggesting that individuals are paid to use the centre, however this would dramatically enhance the usage figures, but you could consider linking some kind of financial reward to an individual's efforts to develop themselves. If, for example, they have demonstrated that as a direct result of using the learning centre their ability to perform their job has improved, in whatever capacity, they should be rewarded.

There are several advantages to adopting this scheme, the first being that it will encourage individuals to use the centre, and to take self-development seriously; it will also act as an incentive for their line managers to provide you with accurate feedback on the value of the centre; and it will also give you more evidence to justify the learning centre to the board and to push for a larger budget. The organization invests in development largely because it wants to increase the overall performance of individual staff, and if you can prove that this is happening as a direct result of the facilities that the centre provides then you can make your own shopping list.

I am not the only one who believes in this kind of reward scheme. Peter Honey is also a strong advocate of 'learning-related pay', and stated quite bluntly in an article that 'when it comes to something as important as learning, we need to put our money where our mouth is' ('Performance-related pay should include learning-related pay', *Training Officer*, 32, 8, October 1996).

Learning sets

As the move towards self-development is such a dramatic shift people will need support and encouragement; a great deal of motivation is required for an individual to get up and go to the learning centre, and this is where setting up learning networks can be of enormous value. These networks can be formally organized or informal gatherings. The aim is to provide individuals with a mechanism to get together to share their experiences; they can, for example, be set up for managers in order that they have a forum within which people can discuss ideas and initiatives that have worked for them.

Many organizations are already implementing these forms of groups to provide managers with some kind of support; but what they are also quite cleverly doing is ensuring that the managers are supporting themselves rather than being spoon-fed by the training department. During these forums the managers are encouraged to work out the answers for themselves; no one is telling them what or how to do things – they are experiencing it for themselves. If you take this route the most difficult hurdle you will come up against will be getting the managers to commit themselves to giving up their time to attend the meetings. Some organizations have imposed this upon managers, making sure that development becomes a regular feature at each of their area meetings. However, we all know that this is almost impossible to monitor, and all too often the day-to-day issues will take precedence and development will take a back seat.

I believe that a separate meeting is the best solution if you want to ensure that these issues are really discussed. But in order for this to happen the managers need to fully understand the importance of training, and because the effects are not always instantly recognized this is not always easy to do. Offering managers some form of reward or incentive can help overcome this potential hurdle; however involvement is always a good sweetener, as is competition. It may be an idea to arrange for the individual managers to visit another organization's learning centre, or you could encourage them to visit an organization where the individual managers really do assist in the training and development function. It may act as a complete eye-opener, and it will also give them the opportunity to see exactly what is happening outside of their own working environment, dispelling the myth that it is not just their own organization that is encouraging them to take this route.

The future of the learning centre

I expect that the change in the role of training and development will continue – we have already seen a dramatic shift in the way in which organizations are developing their staff. More and more responsibility is being handed to the line manager, the trainer's role is becoming that of a support mechanism, and the learning centre is providing the tools for facilitated learning approaches. But will it continue? This is not an easy question to answer, and perhaps it should not be answered at all. If we concern ourselves too much with changes in the future we will not dedicate the time and energy to getting it right in the present.

Learning centres are becoming an integral part of the development process, but it is up to the individual to decide to what extent this expands. It may be that in five years' time the learning centre as we know it today will be obsolete, replaced with other forms of technology like the Intranet where people will not even have to move away from their desks to receive training. But what will always be a necessity is the support and feedback that an individual will need to receive, and the question is, can technology ever provide this?

The future therefore lies in a change in behaviour and a shift in the responsibility of the individual. This change cannot take place overnight or indeed in a few months – the learning centre is a stepping-stone in the process to creating a true learning environment, and to achieve this effectively time and commitment needs to be spent on the process.

Chapter 13

Case studies

Royal Marsden NHS Trust

The Royal Marsden has had great success with its two learning centres based in London and Surrey; the organization which currently employees 1500 staff set up the initial site at Sutton in August 1995. The reasons behind the implementation of the learning centres were the comments from individual members of staff and the training department being made aware that it was becomingly increasingly difficult to release staff to attend formally run courses. In addition to this the Marsden wanted to provide individuals with some form of support for the NVQ diplomas and certificates that they were undertaking. It was not only a strategic decision, but one which was identified by the individual staff members themselves. As it was the training department that had identified the need there was no need to sell the concept to the department, and fortunately it received a great deal of support from the human resources Director, who was the main sponsor and the director of facilities, who helped them find a suitable location. The manner in which the concept of self-development and open learning was sold is described by Amanda Wade – Assistant Director, Management and Organisational Development – as a 'trickle effect'. The Royal Marsden did not conduct a major launch for several reasons: it wanted to familiarize itself with the resources and the equipment; it also realized its own limitations and did not want to stretch itself.

In order to avoid the problem of overstocking on resources, the Marsden started off by making the facilities available to a select few, so that it could monitor the demand more effectively, initially the centre was only advertised to a few employees via mail shots with study leave confirmation letters. However, due to the success of the first centre in Sutton, the second one in Chelsea was launched with newsletters, and a Guide to Services was produced which outlined all of the courses available. A working party was not set up at the Marsden but a great deal of research went into sourcing hardware/software providers in order that the best deals could be achieved, once costings had been made the proposal was put to the senior management team. Following this the next step was to locate a suitable site. The one chosen was at the time an old staff flat, which was later converted into an office for the centre adviser, a room for multimedia PCs, a study room, a kitchenette and equal access toilet.

The Royal Marsden's set-up process

October 1994	Ideas formed about the project
February 1995	Research began into providers and cost, proposal put to senior management

May 1995	Proposal agreed by senior management and budget identified
End May 1995	Hardware and software purchased from one supplier
August 1995	Sutton centre location identified and building work commenced
September 1995	Move to Sutton site – staff informed of facilities
December 1995	Suitable locations researched for Chelsea site
January 1996	Usage at Sutton site 50 per cent
March 1995	Usage at Sutton 75 per cent
June 1996	Accommodation at Chelsea identified, and building work begun.
September 1996	Move to Chelsea site – staff informed of facilities

Set-up costs

£40,000 was spent on resources and hardware, giving 70 CD-ROM, interactive video and linear video packages. Additional 'current' issue packages have been purchased as necessary.

Resources

In terms of the types of media the Marsden decided to opt for a mix of media which enabled it to provide resources to suit all learning styles, and it would appear that this has proved very effective. The areas of resources that are covered within the centre include some of the following:

- management and supervisory skills
- communication skills
- health and safety
- PC skills.

The centres are currently previewing non-vocational materials to assess their suitability. The range of PC packages on offer complement the existing trainer-led courses run by the Trust's computing department. Students appreciate an alternative mechanism through which to develop IT skills, particularly the more basic ones, such as how to use a personal computer.

Obstacles

It was not all plain sailing for the Royal Marsden, particularly during the early stages. As space was at a premium it took five months to locate the first site and 17 for the second. It also found that the whole project took a lot longer than it had originally anticipated. The only other obstacle was quite minor in relation to other organizations – a few teething problems with the equipment.

Benefits

The Royal Marsden believes that the benefits of the centre to the organization have been extensive, the prime benefit being one of cost. It has monitored the usage of the centres and found that they enable many people to develop various skills, one of the most popular being PC skills, and this has saved enormous amounts of money by not having to put individuals through specific IT training courses, which are often not as effective as self-development tools. It has also received feedback stating that many like the privacy of the learning centre, which allows them to learn at their own pace. Another benefit has been the time element – people are able to develop in shorter, more frequent bursts, which means that they do not have to be away from the office for long periods of time. This is of course good news for the line manager, but also means that the individual does not have a mountain of work to return to and eliminates the amount of stress that this can cause.

Administration

Lorraine Stanley, the Training and Development Adviser, is responsible for the day-to-day running of both centres. This is her primary role and as such she is able to dedicate most of her time and energy to the effective maintenance of the centres. At the moment she is obliged to split her time between the two centres; however as soon as the second centre is more established and usage has reached a reasonable level a second administrator will be employed. It has been demonstrated at the Royal Marsden that a key factor for success is the provision of student support, and the ownership by one person of the promotion of the centres. The main areas of Lorraine's role include:

- running induction programmes
- advising managers and staff on suitable packages for their training needs
- dealing with any technical problems
- liaising with suppliers
- supporting students
- recommending new products for the centre.

Induction

New users of the centre must undertake a one-hour induction course which is facilitated by the Training and Development

Adviser. This process ensures that all new members are aware of how to use the equipment correctly, thus reducing the amount of time that the adviser must spend with users who suffer teething problems.

Logistics

The centre is currently administered on paper. However, due to ever-increasing usage, a software package for training administration is being set up, to help allocate and monitor resource use. The Marsden only loans out video-based material, and if people want to borrow videos they must come in personally to collect them; these are then signed for in order that they can be traced effectively.

Security

New students can only use the centre when an administrator is there. However, keys are made available for 'mature' students to access their packages and machinery out of hours, or when staff are involved in other activities. At present all the materials are locked away at night and hardware is secured to the desks with a bolt.

Who uses the centre?

Analysis shows that a range of people are making use of the centre from all professions and departments. However, only a small number of senior managers is using the facility.

How many people use the centre?

The centre is still in its early days, and the average attendance is between six and eight each day.

How is it marketed?

As the Marsden is quite happy with the usage (and has waiting lists) it has not felt that a great deal of marketing is essential, but this is not say that it does not take place. The main tools for marketing the facility are the Guide to Services, the newsletter and 'come and try it' sessions in the dining-room.

How are employees encouraged to develop themselves within the organization?

The Royal Marsden encourages all staff to develop in their roles and beyond. Development is aligned with the achievement of individual, department and corporate objectives. Staff are supported with 100 per cent finance if a course is job related, 75 per cent for training which is combined job and personal development. Coaching and mentoring is also encouraged and objectives are regularly set.

What aided the success of the centre?

The Marsden was fortunate in that it received commitment from the senior managers at an early stage. It also set itself realistic objectives – deciding to start small and grow slowly in order that it could learn how to use the equipment effectively. This also enabled it to become familiar with the resources and cope with the increasing demand. It also did not declare the centre a success until it was certain that it was.

London Ambulance Service

London Ambulance Service (LAS), based at Waterloo, opened its learning centre on 16 April 1996. This centre has also proved to be a success with all 3000 staff having access to the training centre based in Bromley. This site was intended as a pilot and two others are due to open in the early part of next year, both servicing the London area. As the training department was responsible for the set up there was no real conflict created.

The reason for opening was the result of a strategic decision, another step towards the LAS becoming a learning organization. The Training and Development Manager, Tom Martin-Herbert, wanted people to have the opportunity to continue their learning, but recognized that people required the resources to do this. The next step was to sell the concept to the directors, and of course to gain funding for the project; fortunately support was won very early on and as a result Tom and his team were able to start planning the project.

The initial step was to set up a working party. The team felt that by doing this it would be able to delegate tasks to sub-working parties, and would be able to get a mixed range of views from individuals from different departments and levels. It did not want to restrict the working party to the training team and a conscious effort was made not to do so. The decision on who to include in the team was made through discussions with the training team, and following this the relevant people were approached and the working party set up. It met monthly on a formal basis and also met to discuss relevant issues when necessary. Before taking the plunge, the working party visited other open learning centres within a range of sectors to see how they had been set up and how they were managed. It felt that these visits gave a good insight into the problems that other organizations had encountered. The visits also gave the working party ideas on the layout of the centre, and how it wanted the LAS centre to look.

The first step

The team decided that it wanted to gauge people's reactions to the learning centre – this was considered a very important area. It wanted to ensure that the materials held within the centre would be of value to the users, and it was decided that the only way to assess this was through the development of a questionnaire. The questionnaire was mailed to all staff and was colour coded – different colours represented different departments – which enabled the team to evaluate the results with greater ease. The questionnaire covered various issues, for example:

■ Would you support the learning resource centre?
■ What areas would you like the materials to cover?
■ What media would you like to see within the centre?

People were given a strict deadline within which to return the completed questionnaire; the return rate was 18 per cent.

The London Ambulance Service's set-up process

April 1995	Open learning centre proposal researched
May 1995	Working party set up
Mid-May	Questionnaire designed and distributed among staff
June 1995	Questionnaires returned and analysed
July 1995	Hardware purchased
July 1995	Refurbishment of room commenced
December 1995	Purchasing of resources

January 1996   Catalogue completed

March 1996   Room completed

April 1996   Official launch

Environment/layout

Fortunately a room was allocated for the learning centre very early on, and its location was ideal as it was situated at the training centre in Bromley. The responsibility for the room was left to a sub-working party; unfortunately there was a lot of work to be done on the room as it was felt that it was not conducive to learning at all. The environment was extremely important to the team, as it was essential that people felt comfortable there and that it was somewhere they would actually enjoy studying. As a consequence a lot of time was dedicated to getting it just right, and there was much discussion over the colour of the room, the furniture and the overall layout. The team took their ideas from other learning centres they had seen; one idea which came from attending a seminar was the use of 'piped' music within the learning centre. The team felt it was important to create a 'calming' environment, one in which people would feel they could get away. This was particularly important as most of the users work in very stressful, reactive conditions, and it is not often they get the opportunity to escape from the telephone or the highly pressurized environments to which they are accustomed. The team recognized this need and as such created a very soft, soothing effect within the centre.

Cost

The total cost of setting up the centre was between £60,000 and £80,000. Approximately 50 per cent of this figure included resources, the remainder covered hardware, furnishing the room and marketing.

Media

The choice of media was based on the responses to the questionnaire and the need to cover all learning styles, so a mix of media
was chosen. The team also wanted materials to be included that
the trainers could use so a selection of games was incorporated
together with activity manuals. The decision to use CD-I was
made as the team felt that it fitted mid-way between CD-ROM
and video, the trainers could use it and it would be used by
those who were so-called 'technophobes'. The centre currently
has the following hardware:

- Five multimedia stations
- Three videos and TVs
- Two CD-I players.

Resources

Resources were chosen again on the basis of the results of the
questionnaire together with other needs that had been identified
by the training team. An independent organization was also used,
which was responsible for identifying the most suitable resources
and for the development of a catalogue which was then distributed to the users. All materials were evaluated for suitability by
the team over a period of three months. The team decided to
include a selection of non-vocational materials, and these
resources covered a wide area – from languages to antique
purchasing and cookery. The reason for this was to provide
materials that were not directly linked to people's jobs, the team
wanted individuals to feel that the centre was there for them,
not only as a means of increasing their effectiveness within the
workplace. It also helped stimulate usage. Other areas that have

proved popular were the IT materials, in particular the more basic material that covered PC awareness.

The launch

The launch was quite a formal, all-day affair, with 50 attendees. The morning was only open to people who were formally invited, the reason for this decision being lack of space – there was not certainly not enough room to accommodate 3000 people. The centre was opened by the chairman of the LAS who was shown around with other senior managers.

The afternoon was open house for all employees. The team were a little disappointed with the numbers who attended but felt that this was due to work commitments. Despite lack of attendance the launch was declared a success, and it was felt that this was largely due to the fact that no one had access to the centre prior to the launch, this gave people a sense of excitement, not knowing what to expect. Promotional materials were given out on the day, each person received a pen with the telephone number and logo of the centre printed on.

Administration

A full-time administrator was in place prior to the launch of the centre, her role being to administer the centre; her responsibilities do not include the marketing of the centre. Her main task is to book people into the centre, show them how to use the equipment and provide them with help and assistance when they are in the centre.

Logging out resources

Each person who uses the centre is allocated a membership card with a unique number. Each time they ask to book resources out of the centre they must leave their membership card behind, details of the loan are then logged against the card. It then becomes the responsibility of the administrator to ensure that the materials are returned on time, ie within the three-week period that they are allocated.

How are the materials sent out?

The materials are either sent to the customer via internal post or are delivered by hand by the in-service trainer.

Security

The centre is secured with steel shutters, the windows have reflective glass and security doors have been fitted.

Opening hours

The centre is currently open from 8am to 6pm, during which time there is always someone available to deal with customers, whether this be the administrator or a trainer.

Usage

The centre has approximately six users per day, but it is felt that this will increase quite dramatically when it is marketed more.

Marketing

The team plans to send posters advertising the centre to all departments, which will be sent out via the in-service trainers. Most of the marketing is done via face-to-face selling at present, and all new recruits are shown around the centre.

Future role of the centre

The team would like the centre to have greater links with the more formal courses, as it feels that there needs to be a network established in which pre-course work is takes place within the centre. It is also planning to develop its own in-house, computer-based training packages for more technical training.

In retrospect, the only thing they feel that they should have done differently is to have involved more senior managers, particularly within the working party.

How is it evaluated?

The working party that was initially set up is still in existence and is now responsible for the monitoring of the current centre; it is also their responsibility to assess usage and to evaluate future needs.

Is it a success?

Yes, it has proved to be a great success, with more divisions within the service requesting their own learning centre facility. Although no dedicated evaluation has been done, there has been a noticeable increase in the pass rates on the technical side and this is felt to be a direct result of the learning centre.

Virgin Atlantic Airways

The need for a learning centre was identified by both the cabin crew training team and staff. It was felt that the existing training covered the essential areas but once staff have gone through the initial six-week course they are only asked back for the statutory safety training courses. The staff and the training team felt that individuals needed the opportunity to develop themselves further, but they faced a huge obstacle. Given the nature of their jobs people work all hours and are very rarely in the same location, making it difficult for people to receive more formalized training. As a consequence it was decided that a learning centre could be the perfect solution. A team was not put in place, the main driving force behind the project was one of the cabin crew training team. The project fortunately did not need much selling, as it was a need that had been identified by both the crew and the training team.

Selling the concept

The only people who needed convincing was the Board of Directors, and the only reservations they had concerned cost. This obstacle was soon overcome by the proposal that the team put forward. The first step was to identify the reactions of the cabin crew and this was assessed by way of a questionnaire that was sent to 1200 employees, the return was estimated at 12 per cent. The questionnaire covered a range of issues, the main area being what subjects the cabin crew would like to centre to include.

Virgin Atlantic Airways' set-up process

July 1995	Need identified and proposal put to the board
August 1995	Research commenced – visits to other learning centres and independent advice sought
September 1995	Questionnaires distributed
November 1995	Move to new location, room allocated
December 1995	Research into resources and media
January 1996	Materials assessed
February 1996	Centre launched

Media

The decision relating to media was linked to the needs that had been identified by the crew together with those of the training team, and a mix of media was chosen in order to match a variety of learning styles and preferences. All the resources were evaluated prior to purchasing at an independent resource centre. This was quite a time-consuming process, but one which Virgin felt necessary as they wanted to ensure that the material would be used by the crew. A decision was also made to include other resources that covered non-vocational issues, languages being one of these; however, language learning could be classed as vocational due to the nature of the crew's role. They also purchased material which covered the following areas:

■ how to plan a wedding
■ DIY
■ calligraphy

- gardening
- history
- law
- photography
- travel guides
- health and well-being
- media.

The launch

The official launch was attended by Richard Branson, Chairman, and Steve Ridgeway, Customer Services Director, together with other senior managers. The launch was a formal affair that took place over two days, this was necessary due to the irregular working hours of the crew. The launch was a high-profile event as one might imagine, and had a party-like atmosphere with balloons, streamers etc. The launch was intended to act as a medium through which people could gain a greater understanding of the objective of the learning centre, and to show people exactly how it could be of benefit to them.

Due to the nature of the crew's jobs, the number of attendees was relatively low, as many were away on trips. However, this has not affected the success of the centre in any way.

Staffing

This has proved to be one of the biggest factors influencing the usage rate of the centre. An administrator was not employed from the outset, and as a consequence the running of the centre became part of the responsibility of one of the trainers, David Innes. As a result of his dual role he has not been able to dedicate the time and energy that he feels the centre deserves. Fortunately help is at hand and a member of the cabin crew has been seconded to the centre; David is sure that this will have a quite dramatic effect on the levels of use and will enable him to concentrate on marketing the centre, which he feels has not really been achieved successfully.

Usage

At the moment the centre receives approximately ten customers a day. This is not a particularly high figure, however, and work is being done to increase this via internal promotion campaigns. One barrier that David feels is preventing increase in usage is the fact that currently materials are not loaned out. This is due to change as soon as they have installed the administration software package 'Resource Manager', which will enable them to keep track of all the resources as well as make bookings and run reports on usage.

Opening hours

The centre is open from 9am to 5.30pm, but it is felt that the opening hours do not necessarily suit the potential users and as soon as it is possible the opening hours will increase.

Who uses it?

As expected, the centre's biggest customers are the cabin crew, at whom the centre was originally targeted. Since the centre has been opened up company-wide, a small percentage of middle managers have also made use of the facility and it is hoped that more will do so in the future.

Marketing

When the centre was launched it was promoted by way of a poster campaign, which proved quite effective in getting the initial message across, and as a consequence the same tactic will be employed to promote it again. The centre is also featured in the company newsletter, and every new recruit is issued with a catalogue and introductory brochure. Staff looking for promotion or for a new job within the company are encouraged to use the facilities in the centre via a reminder on all staff vacancy notices.

Victoria and Albert Museum

The museum set up a learning centre which was launched on 30 May 1996. The museum, based in South Kensington, London, has 850 employees, and the decision to set up a learning centre was due to the change in culture that the museum wanted to create. It wanted to instil a culture of 'lifetime learning' within the organization whereby individuals would have the opportunity to develop. It also realized that an alternative to the more traditional training courses needed to be provided in order to cater for the wide range of learning styles. The centre would also enable the museum to provide support and assistance for professional development programmes, as well as provide the staff with a wider range of options that would enable them to obtain the necessary skills that would, in turn, help them meet the objectives of the museum.

The main driving force behind the project was the training section within the museum, with support from the head of personnel and assistant director (administration). As such a high level of personnel was behind the project wholeheartedly the budget did not prove difficult to receive, and the task was also made easier by the fact that the training centre was being moved to a new site with a room already allocated for the learning centre.

As the concept did not need to be sold to the senior managers the only task that remained was to sell the idea to the employees. The museum did this by involving them from the earliest opportunity by asking for their feedback by way of the questionnaire (see below). In addition to this, as the centre was about to launch all staff were issued with a leaflet which explained what the centre was and how it could be used.

Market research

In order to assess the needs of the employees the training team issued a questionnaire which asked the employees what kinds of materials they would like the resource centre to contain, and whether they were likely to make use of the facility. The questionnaire was sent to all staff and 160 forms were returned, this in itself demonstrating the extent of interest within the employee base.

Set-up cost

The training department already had a substantial number of resources which were subsequently allocated to the centre, and the museum received a grant from the local Training and Enterprise Council for £5000. This enabled them to purchase a multimedia station and have allocated the remaining £3000 for further resources. The initial budget was by no means huge, but this has not prevented the museum from establishing a well-used centre.

Media

This was chosen both as a result of replies to the initial questionnaire and the desire to address different learning styles. The museum did not want to stick with the more traditionally based open learning resources, but wanted to update technology, which is why the decision to have a multimedia station was made. The centre currently provides the following:

■ One multimedia station
■ Two video/CD-I players.

Resources

Due to the limited budget not all areas of need could be covered, but the ones which had been identified as 'must haves' were purchased, and these include the following:

- management
- personal development
- interpersonal skills
- report writing
- languages
- museology (the study/practice of museums)
- dealing with the public
- health and safety
- computer skills.

As can be seen from the above list, the decision was made to include a selection of non-vocational materials. These have proved to be a worthy investment, one of the most popular materials being those linked to IT skills' development.

The launch

All staff were invited to the official launch, 30 of whom actually attended, and a great deal of interest was shown in the materials in the centre. The format of the launch was a lunchtime event, with refreshments provided for those who attended. While the actual number of attendees was relatively small in comparison to other organizations the Victoria and Albert felt that it was a success. They had expected approximately this number and, as the centre is quite small a larger number would have made access rather difficult. The objective of the launch was to spend quality time with individuals, enabling the team to discuss individuals' needs and how the centre could meet them. The museum also felt that the launch was only a tiny part in the process of ongoing awareness that needed to be accomplished through other marketing mechanisms.

In addition to the launch other initiatives were put in place that provided the team with the opportunity to show people around the centre, one of these being the new performance management system. Showing people around the learning centre then became an integral part of the course, with staff having the opportunity to see exactly how it could be used.

Opening hours

The centre is open from 8.30am to 5.30pm daily, but these hours can be extended by prior arrangement.

Administration

At present there is no full-time administrator, a member of the training team has responsibility for manning the centre. Her responsibilities include:

- booking in delegates
- discussing their needs
- providing reports
- publicizing the centre
- purchasing new material.

Usage

Since its opening the centre has had 80 individuals through the doors, many of whom return on a regular basis. In addition, over 70 items have been loaned out.

Marketing

As the centre is situated within the training centre all delegates have to pass it, and it is hoped to generate interest in this way. Most of the marketing takes the form of word of mouth but also by integrating the idea of the centre into the more formal tutor-led training sessions.

Evaluation

Very little evaluation has yet been conducted and there are no formal structures in place to obtain it. However there are plans to distribute a questionnaire to the users to ask them if they feel the centre has helped them in their work and how it could be improved.

Heathrow Airport Ltd

Heathrow Airport Limited employ between 3500 and 4000 staff and set up its central learning centre in March 1995. The decision to set up a learning centre was based on a need which was identified through a staff survey, the results of which indicated that employees wanted greater access to a wider range of subjects, and it was felt that the most effective way of addressing this was through the development of an open learning centre. The main driving force behind the centre was the training manager, in conjunction with the head of personnel and the managing director. As the need was identified by the staff themselves there was no reason to sell the concept to them, and fortunately support was available from the senior managers from the outset.

The decision to set up a learning centre was seen as a very positive one by the training department as they had requested such a facility for a number of years. The management, on the other hand, while feeling positive about the provision of the facility, did not really understand the concept and this was therefore an area that the training department needed to tackle. The reaction of the employees was as expected quite mixed. Some felt that the centre was just another training 'gimmick', while others embraced the idea wholeheartedly.

Once the go-ahead had been given the first step was to do some research, and this was achieved by the person responsible for the project attending a one-day seminar on setting up learning centres. In addition several existing learning centres were visited. Following this the second stage was to set up a project team or working party.

The Training Manager John Prior, who was responsible for the project, realized that his particular skills lay within IT systems and general organizational, so he enlisted the assistance of personnel trainers to look at the course subjects and personnel officers to look at the delivery methods. The working party numbered six in total, not all of whom were involved in all aspects of setting up the centre but certainly had a part to play in its development.

The set-up procedure

The procedure was as follows:

- accommodation identified – visits made to other OLCs
- decisions made on courseware and technology
- furniture chosen and ordered
- hardware and courseware ordered
- setting up and testing of hardware/software
- administration system put in place
- course catalogues produced
- brochures distributed to all staff
- posters put on noticeboards
- open days organized.

Location

In January 1995 Heathrow Airport Limited acquired a new training suite, and fortunately provision for the learning centre was made. Several months later four satellite learning centres were also established, each of these being located in the passenger terminals. The reason for the satellite centres was to overcome the problem of distance that employees were encountering by having to travel to the main OLC site.

Environment/layout

The team worked against a set criteria: minimum size of room' number of workstations, lighting, security, booking system. It tried not to be too rigid but wanted to maintain very general guidelines. As with most organizations space was at a premium and often the team had to make do with what it was given.

Cost

In total £70,000 was spent; £40,000 on the main site and the remainder on the satellites. This cost included:

- hardware
- furniture
- courseware
- support.

Media

The decision was made to have a mix of media within the centres, the emphasis being placed largely on the quality of the resources, and a good amount of time was devoted to its selection. The main centre has eight multimedia stations and the satellite centres two multimedia stations each.

Resources

The materials were selected against the needs that had been identified by the staff themselves and those that the training team had become aware of. As a result the resources covered a wide range of skills and included some non-vocational areas. Ten per cent of the resources contained within the centres are non-vocational, and it is felt that their inclusion has encouraged staff to use the centre and has aided the selling process.

The launch

The launch took place over a period of two days and took the format of open days rather than a formal launch ceremony. It was promoted by using a variety of communication methods which included posters, e-mail and brochures (given out with pay slips).

A total of 6 per cent of the employee base attended over the two days, and while the team felt that it would have been nice to have had a greater attendance it was not by any means demoralized. It felt that the launch had succeeded in achieving its objective, which was to get the initial message across to employees.

Administration

The centre does not have a full-time administrator. Bookings are made through the training centre administration, technical support is the responsibility of the training manager, and daily support is the responsibility of the personnel officers and trainers. A database has been created internally which facilitates bookings, and also lends itself to the production of reports if required.

Security

There is a monitoring system in place at each of the sites and all resources are locked away unless they are being used. No resources are loaned out.

Opening hours

The main centre is open from 8am to 5pm Monday to Friday; the satellite centres are open 24 hours a day, seven days a week.

Usage

Six staff per day use the facilities for a maximum of four hours each. The main users tend to be support staff with a few middle managers.

Growth

The main centre has reduced in size, due to the fact that the satellite centres have increased. Despite this it would seem that the overall usage figures have decreased since the opening.

Marketing

The facility is marketed internally largely through word of mouth and by e-mail, bulletin boards and posters.

The future of the learning centre

The centre will soon be used to train users on new software applications that will be adopted by the organization, necessitating the training of some 2000 employees. This will of course increase usage dramatically and will also provide an opportunity for staff to be sold the concept of self-development. In addition to this particular initiative it has been noted that more departments are requesting their own facilities and it is felt that a move to having open learning closer to the working environment will continue. Plans are also being made to develop courseware to enhance the number of programmes currently available and to make these available to all staff via the Internet.

What would they have done differently?

It is felt that the centre requires a full-time administrator to really make the most of the facility, and that having joint responsibilities has not given the users the service that they need in order to make the centre as effective as it has the potential to be. Aside from this the team felt that the centres were set up in a very efficient manner, which resulted in a certain degree of success. There is still a lot more work to be done before the team can say that it has been a totally successful open learning culture; but on the other hand the need was only identified two years ago and there are now five open learning centres which have effectively met their customers' needs.

SIMS Education Services Ltd

SIMS is a software house with a small employee base of only 280. However, this did not prevent them from taking the decision to set up a learning centre facility in 1994. The reason behind this decision was that the personnel manager, with the backing of senior managers, felt that there needed to be a provision for staff to study other than at home or on a course; they also wanted to link development to the personal review process, believing that managers needed to turn somewhere for support and that the centre could provide them with this.

A project team was not put together as the centre was to be on a very small scale, and the only problem that the personnel manager Bob Creedy encountered during the early stages was knowing what to purchase. At that time open learning centres were a relatively new concept, and the amount of information and guidance available to him was minimal. As a consequence he made use of an independent supplier who gave him advice and assistance in choosing the resources.

Cost

In total, the centre cost £13,000 to set up:

- hardware   £3,000
  (this consisted of a multimedia PC, CD-I player/monitor, video recorder/television, cassette player, and headphones)
- resources   £10,000

Resources

While there was no formal assessment (ie by way of question-naire), staff were asked what they would like to see in the centre on a more informal basis. The materials were chosen to complement other areas of training and general personal development needs. A mix of media was chosen which included video, text-based resources and technology-based training. A high level of the initial resource costs went on purchasing video and CBT items. The CD-I format has proved something of a dead end with the advent of more sophisticated CD-ROM packages, which employees in our industry can access via their own machines at home. A large proportion of the resources are highly interactive, with a substantial number of workbook-based resources. A decision was made not to include any non-vocational materials – this was largely due to budgetary constraints and space limitations.

The launch

The launch was not a high profile event by any means, again this was partly due to the size of the centre. However it was felt that staff needed to be aware of the facility so quite a large amount of promotional work was undertaken. This included posters, presentations at staff meetings, and regularly publishing updated resources lists.

Administration

The centre does not have a full-time administrator, but is the responsibility of both the personnel manager and an administrator. The administrator is responsible for taking bookings and these are done through the in-house library software. The administrator is not dedicated solely to the resources centre, having other duties, which take up a significant amount of her time. This presents problems in administering and promoting the centre.

Usage

On average two people make use of the centre each day; most of the users are support staff rather than the management. This is area in which Bob Creedy would like to see change, and he feels that the lack of usage is due to the lack of time that he and his administrator are able to dedicate to the centre. The centre is used both for study purposes, being a reasonably quiet oasis in a busy working environment, but also as a review point, where staff can briefly review videos, CD-ROMs etc, before booking them out. Staff not based in head office have access to the resources but geography can impose constraints on their use of them.

Marketing

The centre is marketed but not on a regular basis, and again it is felt that this definitely needs improvement. At present staff are made aware of the facility through the use of posters and information letters, and recently lunchtime seminars have been held on 'Resources for managers', with the idea that this would make them aware of the facilities and resources that are available to them.

What would SIMS have done differently?

The centre would have had a much higher profile with a dedicated full-time administrator to run it more effectively. More work was needed to increase the level of understanding among senior managers at the highest level. Without this, as with most initiatives, it is likely that it will be viewed as peripheral and central to staff development. A resource centre is a cost-effective way of delivering training and development to staff. It is fairly expensive to establish, and without enthusiastic senior support may be subject to close examination if its use is not well proven. While Bob Creedy is happy that the centre is up and running he is not confident that it has been a complete success; he is very aware of the need for continual marketing but does not currently have sufficient resources to do this. He is also aware that until the centre is linked integrally to the review process, usage will remain limited, and feels that there is an immediate need to change this situation.

Appendix I
Forms and questionnaires

SAMPLE LEARNING MATERIAL EVALUATION FORM

(1)

LEARNING MATERIALS REVIEW
FEEDBACK FORM

Reviewed by: ⎯⎯⎯⎯⎯⎯⎯⎯⎯⎯⎯⎯⎯⎯⎯⎯⎯⎯⎯⎯⎯⎯⎯⎯⎯

Organization: ⎯⎯⎯⎯⎯⎯⎯⎯⎯⎯⎯⎯⎯⎯⎯⎯⎯⎯⎯⎯⎯⎯⎯⎯

Date reviewed: ⎯⎯⎯⎯⎯⎯⎯⎯⎯⎯⎯⎯⎯⎯⎯⎯⎯⎯⎯⎯⎯⎯⎯

Place reviewed: ⎯⎯⎯⎯⎯⎯⎯⎯⎯⎯⎯⎯⎯⎯⎯⎯⎯⎯⎯⎯⎯⎯⎯

Type of review: Full use ☐

Detailed review ☐

Key sections plus general overview ☐

Quick overview ☐

Media: Video ☐

CD-ROM ☐

CD-I ☐

Audio ☐

Workbook ☐

Book ☐

Internet module ☐

Title: ⎯⎯⎯⎯⎯⎯⎯⎯⎯⎯⎯⎯⎯⎯⎯⎯⎯⎯⎯⎯⎯⎯⎯⎯⎯⎯⎯⎯

Date produced (if known): ⎯⎯⎯⎯⎯⎯⎯⎯⎯⎯⎯⎯⎯⎯⎯⎯⎯⎯

Produced by: ⎯⎯⎯⎯⎯⎯⎯⎯⎯⎯⎯⎯⎯⎯⎯⎯⎯⎯⎯⎯⎯⎯⎯⎯⎯

Origin: ⎯⎯⎯⎯⎯⎯⎯⎯⎯⎯⎯⎯⎯⎯⎯⎯⎯⎯⎯⎯⎯⎯⎯⎯⎯⎯⎯⎯⎯

Language: ⎯⎯⎯⎯⎯⎯⎯⎯⎯⎯⎯⎯⎯⎯⎯⎯⎯⎯⎯⎯⎯⎯⎯⎯⎯⎯⎯

Approximate learning time of module: ⎯⎯⎯⎯⎯⎯⎯⎯⎯⎯⎯⎯

Key learning areas (refer to Bee-list for guidance): ⎯⎯⎯⎯⎯⎯

⎯⎯⎯⎯⎯⎯⎯⎯⎯⎯⎯⎯⎯⎯⎯⎯⎯⎯⎯⎯⎯⎯⎯⎯⎯⎯⎯⎯⎯⎯⎯⎯⎯⎯

Are there related modules?   Yes/No
If yes give brief details: _____

_____

Effectiveness: _____

Level: Introductory   ☐

                Intermediate   ☐

                Advanced   ☐

Level of technical language/understanding needed:

                High   ☐

                Medium   ☐

                Low   ☐

Key features (please indicate): _____

_____

List any unique style/learning points and relevance (ie do they
work?): _____

_____

_____

Strengths: _____
Weaknesses: _____
Overall rating (on a scale of 1–10 with 1 being the lowest): _____
Price (if known): _____
Value-for-money assessment: _____

Suitability assessment: _____

Links with other Bee centre products?
(please list and say how, and how well, they fit): _____

_____

_____

SAMPLE LEARNING MATERIAL EVALUATION FORM (2)

Suppliers: LRI/Open Mind/other state: _____

Subject area: _____

Type of material: CD-ROM/video/audio tape/book/booklet

Name of material: _____

Original supplier: _____

ISBN (book only): _____

Material suitable for following groups:

Managers	☐
Sales and marketing	☐
Finance	☐
Computing	☐
HR	☐
Supply/distribution/QC	☐
Admin/secretarial	☐

Comments: _____

_____

Size: CD-ROM – How many modules: _____
        How long: _____
        Video – how long: _____
        Audiotape – how long: _____
        Book – number of pages: _____
        Booklet – number of pages: _____

Cost to company: _____

Value for money: Very good/OK/Poor

Learning value (How clearly is learning message projected?):

        Very good/OK/OK, some reservations (state below)/Poor

Reservations: _____

Assessor's comments: _____

_____

_____

Recommendations: _____

        Purchase now/Purchase later/Reject

Name of assessor (Print name) _____

Date _____

_____

_____

SAMPLE OLC PRELAUNCH QUESTIONNAIRE

LONDON AMBULANCE SERVICE
LEARNING RESOURCE CENTRE QUESTIONNAIRE

Please can you answer the following questions and return the completed questionnaire in the attached envelope to Bromley Training Centre by 1 September.

1. Are you likely to make use of the Learning Resource Centre (LRC)? Yes/No

2. If you answered no, please could you tell us your reason?
   _____
   _____
   _____

3. If yes, please could you indicate how you may use the LRC, tick as many as you want.

Visiting the centre to:

Use the computer-based training equipment ☐

Use the video and/or CD-I materials ☐

Use CD-ROM materials ☐

Read/Refer to books and/or journals ☐

Use open learning materials ☐

Loan from the centre:

Computer-based training packages ☐

Video/CD-I materials ☐

CD-ROM materials ☐

Books ☐

Journals ☐

Open learning materials ☐

4. To be successful the LRC needs to stock a variety of materials in a range of areas. These are the main areas we feel are important. Using the boxes placed by each area, please tick those you agree with, place a cross against those you disagree with or leave blank any you have no strong views on.

Ambulance aid procedures ☐

Pre-paramedic learning materials ☐

Paramedic procedures ☐

Physiology and other related disciplines ☐

General management skills ☐

Computing skills (basic, intermediate, advanced) ☐

Finance/Budget skills ☐

LAS policies and procedures ☐

Administration skills ☐

Professional qualifications ☐

If there are any other subject areas you would like materials provided for, please add them below:

_____

_____

_____

5. What support do you think you would need:

Time to attend centre ☐

Access to Helpline ☐

Access to a 'tutor' to talk through any points ☐

Help forming a 'study group' in particular subjects ☐

Any other support, please list:

_____

_____

_____

6. Please add any other thoughts/comments you have that may help us to provide you with the resources and service you need.

_____

_____

_____

Thank you for taking the time to complete this questionnaire, please could you return it to Bromley Training Centre by 1 September in the envelope provided. We will be publishing the results plus further details in a future issue of *LAS News*.

Appendix II

Recommended reading

Books on learning and study skills

The following is a list of recommended titles on learning and study that could (or perhaps should) be made available to all new members or users of resource-based learning initiatives. Many people will be unused to learning or unsure whether they can get back into a study and learning mode – they need all the help they can get!

Learning Resources International, for example, has developed its own guide to learning, study and self-development. This is in the form of a booklet which organizations are encouraged to provide as part of an introductory welcome pack to new users of learning centres.

Freeman, Richard and Meed, John (1993) *How to Study Effectively*, Learning Skills Series, Collins Educational, London.

Inglis, John and Lewis, Roger (1993) *Clear Thinking*, Learning Skills Series, Collins Educational, London.

Lewis, Roger (1994) *How to Manage Your Study Time*, Learning Skills Series, Collins Educational, London.

Mckeown, Sam (1991) *Developing Learning Skills*, National Extension College, Cambridge.

Pedler, Mike, Burgoyne, John and Boydell, Tom (1994) *A Manager's Guide to Self-Development*, McGraw-Hill, Maidenhead.

Race, Phil, Reddick, Roisin, Sloan, Barry and Vaughan, Judy (1990) *Learning Skills Resource Bank*, National Extension College, Cambridge.

Recommended materials for learning organizations

This is a list of the best available materials for organizations that are (or think they are) moving towards a learning culture.

Grundy, Tony (1994) *Strategic Learning in Action: How to Accelerate and Sustain Business,* Henley Management Series, McGraw-Hill, Maidenhead.

Lessem, Ronnie (1993) *Business as a Learning Community: Applying Global Concepts to,* McGraw-Hill, Maidenhead.

Mayo, Andrew and Lank, Elizabeth (1994) *The Power of Learning,* Developing Strategies Series, Institute of Personnel and Development, London.

Mumford, Alan (1995) *Learning at the Top,* Developing Organisations Series, McGraw-Hill, Maidenhead.

Pedler, Mike, Burgoyne, John and Boydell, Tom (1991) *The Learning Company: A Strategy for Sustainable Development,* McGraw-Hill, Maidenhead.

Senge, Peter M (1993) *The Fifth Discipline: Art and Practice of a Learning Organisation,* Century Business, London.

Senge, Peter M (1993) *The Fifth Discipline Fieldbook: Strategies for Building a Learning Organisation,* Century Business, London.

Wick, Calhoun and Leon, W Stanton (1993) *The Learning Edge,* McGraw-Hill, Maidenhead.

Wood, Sue (ed) (1988) *Continuous Development: The Path to Improved Performance,* Institute of Personnel Management, London.

Learning styles

It is useful, if not essential, for people to understand both their own learning styles and that of others, in order to fully grasp their importance to the learning process.

Brown, Roswyn A (1996) *Learning Skills, Studying Styles and Profiling,* Quay Books, Mark Allen Publishing.

Dudley, Geoffrey A (1986) *Double Your Learning Power: Master the Successful Techniques of Learning and Recall,* Thorsons UK, London.

Honey, Peter and Mumford, Alan (1986) *Using your Learning Styles,* Peter Honey.

Honey, Peter and Mumford, Alan (1992) *Manual of Learning Styles,* Peter Honey.

Lawrence, Gordon (1993) *People Types and Tiger Stripes (A Practical Guide to Learning Styles),* Center for Applications of Psychological Type, US.

Matte, Nancy L (1995) *Success – Your Style! Right and Left Brain Techniques for Learning,* Wadsworth Publishing (Bowker US).

Pues (1993) *Help Yourself: How to Take Advantage of Your Learning Styles,* New Readers, US.

Renzulli, Joseph S (1978) *Learning Styles Inventory: A Measure of Student Preference for Instructional Techniques,* Creative Learning (Bowker US).

Rylatt, Alastair (1994) *Learning Unlimited: Practical Strategies and Techniques for Transforming Learning in the Workplace,* Business and Professional Publishing (Thorpe Au), New South Wales.

Sims, Ronald R (1995) *Importance of Learning Styles: Understanding the Implications for Learning, Course Design and Education,* Greenwood Press, London.

Sims, Ronald R and Sims, Serbrenia J (eds) (1995) *The Importance of Learning Styles,* Greenwood Press, London.

Vail, Priscilla (1992) *Learning Styles: Food for Thought and 130 Practical Tips,* Modern Learning Press, US.

Woodcock, Mike and Francis, Dave P (1994) *Learning Styles Audit,* Management Audit Series, Gower Publishing, Aldershot.

Books aimed at senior management

Champy, James (1996) *Reengineering Management*, HarperCollins, London.

Covey, Stephen R (1990) *The 7 Habits of Highly Effective People*, Macmillan Publishers, Auckland.

Covey, Stephen R, (1992) *Principle-centred Leadership*, Simon & Schuster, Herts.

Covey, Stephen R and Merrill, A Roger, (1993) *First Things First*, Simon & Schuster, Herts.

Drucker, Peter F (1994) *Innovation and Entrepreneurship*, Butterworth-Heinemann, Oxford.

Drucker, Peter F (1995) *The Changing World of the Executive*, Butterworth-Heinemann, Oxford.

Drucker, Peter F (1995) *People and Performance: The Best of Peter Drucker on Management*, Butterworth-Heinemann, Oxford.

Handy, Charles (1995) *The Age of Unreason*, Arrow, Maidenhead.

Handy, Charles (1995) *The Empty Raincoat*, Arrow, Maidenhead.

Handy, Charles (1995) *Gods of Management: The Changing Work of Organisations*, Arrow, Maidenhead.

Kanter, Rosabeth Moss (1985) *The Change Masters: Corporate Entrepreneurs at Work*, International Thomson Business Press, London.

Kanter, Rosabeth Moss (1990) *When Giants Learn to Dance: Mastering the Challenges of Strategy, Management and Careers in the 1990s*, International Thomson Business Press, London.

Obeng, Eddie (1996) *All Change!: The Project Leader's Secret Handbook,* Pitman, London.

Obeng, Eddie and Crainer, Stuart (1995) *Making Re-engineering Happen*, Pitman, London.

Oben, Eddie and Durcan, Jim (1996) *Putting Strategy to Work: A Blueprint for Turning Ideas into Action,* Pitman, London.

Pascale, Richard (1991) *Managing on the Edge: How Successful Companies Use Conflict to Stay Ahead*, Penguin, London.

Peters, Tom and Austin, Nancy (1986) *A Passion for Excellence: The Leadership Difference*, HarperCollins, London.

Peters, Tom and Waterman, Robert H, (1995) *In Search of Excellence: Lessons from America's Best-run Companies*, HarperCollins, London.

Appendix III
Sample catalogue formats

SAMPLE CATALOGUE ENTRY – FORMAT No. 1

MOTIVATION

Title   Motivating the Team

Media   Video and Self-study Workbook (also available on CD-I format)

Date   1995

Length   30 minutes

This video package is aimed at anyone who is responsible for managing a group of people. It will explain by use of Maslow's theory 'What makes people tick'. The video is not theoretical but illustrates through use of drama how you can successfully motivate your staff. The SPUR concept developed by John Mole is used to enable you to identify the need to reward, to appreciate the different needs and requirements individuals have and allow you to build a much more effective team.

Study time   Two hours if workbook used. Anticipate same time for CD-I package.

Suggested activities   Consult members of staff who you feel are motivated and ask them why they are, this can be done by use of inventory or informal consultation.

Speak to other departments within the organization where there is a high percentage of motivated staff and find out what methods are being used to achieve this.

Explore current reward systems that exist within the organization to find out if these suit the particular requirements of your staff, find out what they think of them.

Think about what motivates you! Make a list. Are you motivated? Try a self-assessment questionnaire as suggested.

SAMPLE CATALOGUE ENTRY – FORMAT No. 2

Planning and organization

Title	Media	Publisher	Ref	Summary
Managing Your Time	Audio	Kogan Page	1018	Successful delegation, tackling paperwork, meeting management, handling interruptions, recognizing time-wasting activities and people
The Organised Executive	Audio	Simon & Schuster	1014	
Effective Use of Time	Book	Industrial Society	1153	Practical guide to using time efficiently
Get Organised!	Book	Kogan Page	1173	A guide to personal productivity.
Making Information Work	Book	Open College	1214	How to gather, use and store information. Identifying sources of information and how it is channelled; holding information and where to store it; keeping it secure and confidential
Making the Most of Your Time	Book	Open College	1215	Focusing of priorities, handling paperwork, meetings and other people's demands. A systematic approach to using your time
Managing Time	Book	BPS	1110	The entire process explained, from setting goals to delegating, and from diary control to managing meetings. Two videos plus a game included
Managing Your Time x 3	Book	IPD	1062	Successful delegation, tackling paperwork, meeting management, handling interruptions, recognizing time-wasting activities and people
Win Control of Your Work Day	CBT	Maxim	1196	How to handle constant interruptions by being in control. Techniques for preventing and managing interruptions, strategies for success
Managing Time	Video	BBC	1110	The entire process explained, from setting goals to delegating, and from diary control to managing meetings. Two videos plus a game included
Planning and Organising	Wkbook	Pizza Hut	1002	

SAMPLE CATALOGUE ENTRY – FORMAT No. 3

Motivation

Title	Media	Publisher	Cost
The Motivation Manual	Book	Gower	£25.00

Synopsis
A prize-winning book which takes modern motivational theory and shows how a manager can apply it to create a shared vision and mutual trust.

Title	Media	Publisher	Cost
How to Motivate People	Book	Kogan Page	£5.99
	Audio		£9.99

Synopsis
A practical and easy-to-read guide to help managers improve their skills of motivation.

Title	Media	Publisher	Cost
Successful Motivation in a Week	Book	Hodder	£5.99

Synopsis
A great little guide which takes you through the steps of motivating yourself and your staff.

Title	Media	Publisher	Cost
Chicken Soup for the Soul	Book	US	£10.99

Synopsis
The most powerful book ever compiled – 101 true stories which will change the way you see and do things for ever.

Title	Media	Publisher	Cost
Motivational Quotes	Book	Succesorize	£7.50

Synopsis
Compiled especially for those in sales and management, these quotations are guaranteed to recharge batteries.

Title	Media	Publisher	Cost
Motivational Minutes	Book	Succesorize	£12.95

Synopsis
A collection of clever and compelling ideas which show you how your life can be more meaningful.

Appendix IV

Sample screens from Resource
Manager, OLC Management,
Administration and Reporting System

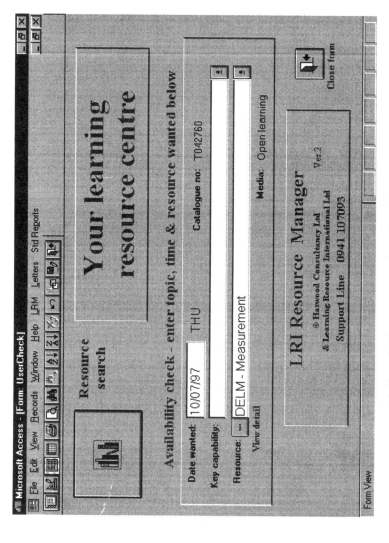

1. *Sample Resource search and availability screen*

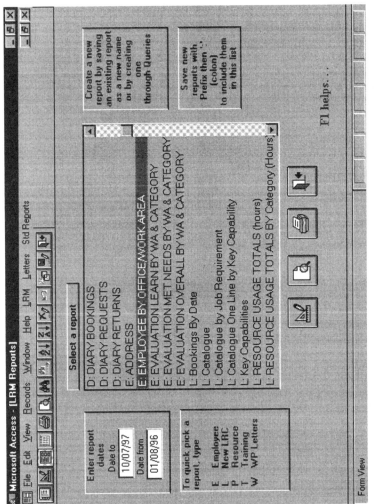

2. *Selection of available reports*

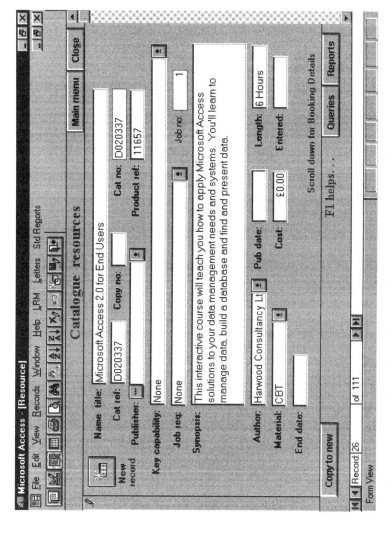

3. *A sample page from the Resources catalogue*

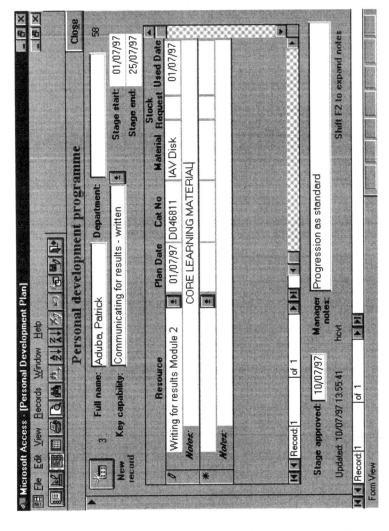

4. Personal Development Programme screen on Resource Manager

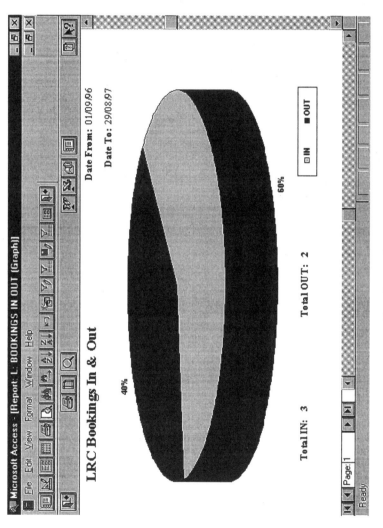

5. *A sample report*

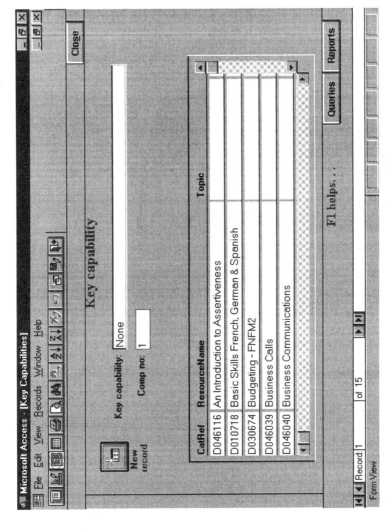

6. *A capability/competency description*

Microsoft Access - [Resource Assessment]

File   Edit   View   Records   Window   Help

Resource evaluation

Resource: Microsoft Windows 3.1 Fundamentals

Book ref: 1280
Cat no: D022928

Full name: Webber. Doug

Evaluation date: 10/07/1997   Used from: 06/02/1997

AssessOld   Close

Please click in the box

	Mainly unsatisfactory	Moderately unsatisfactory	Moderately satisfactory	Mainly satisfactory	Completely satisfactory
Accessibility:			X		
Comfort:				X	
Support:					X
Ease of use of product:				X	
of product:					X
Overall experience:				X	

	Less than 1 hour	1 hour	1 - 2 hours	2-3 hours	More than 3 hours
How long were you in the centre this time				X	

Record: 1   of 1

Form View   FLTR

7. A Resource Assessment screen

Appendix V

Sample OLC Launch Poster

OPEN LEARNING CENTRE

Takes Off 1st May 1996

Virgin Atlantic in association with PBA Training Services invite you to the launch of the Open Learning Centre, VFC, Horley.

We hope that you find the materials on offer both stimulating and enjoyable and they provide a useful aid to your self development.

Please contact David Jones, David Innes or Sam Rasheed on 01293 444 778 for a booking to ensure time in the centre.

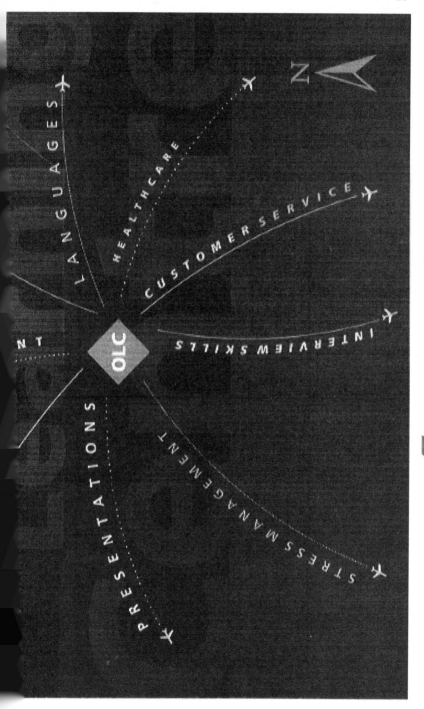

Appendix VI

Resource Manager

A Total

Management

Administration

and Reporting

'Expert' *System*

for

Learning Resource Centres

LRI
LEARNING RESOURCES INTERNATIONAL LTD

What is Resource Manager?
Resource Manager is the only Development Linked, Management, Administration, Reporting and 'Expert' System designed specifically to underpin the running of Learning Centres and Resource Based Learning initiatives and strategies.

Who is it designed for?
Resource Manager has been designed with the following personnel in mind:

● Administrators & Managers of Learning Centres - to provide them with a complete system for running a Centre from booking systems to the creation of 'expertise'.

● Training & HR Managers - to allow them to keep up to date with the current status of the Centre and the progress of individuals and to facilitate the integration of Resource Based Learning elements into the total Training & Development Matrix.

● Line Managers - to encourage their essential support for self development through planning, assessment and involvement.

● Fund Holders - to enable them to receive tailored reports and analyses on the effectiveness of Resource Based Learning Strategies, historically viewed as non-traditional.

● Users of Learning Centres - to enable them to be provided with the sense of support essential to self development initiatives through the enhanced effectiveness of those in a supporting role.

Why was it designed?
Resource Manager was designed after years of involvement with Learning Centres, to answer the need for a comprehensive tool to provide for every aspect of running Learning Centres.

What is an 'Expert' System in this context?
Our experience shows that one of the major restrictions to the success of Learning Centres has been a lack of support for those beginning a process of self development, from the personnel responsible for running the Learning Centre. Faced with a large number of materials and resources covering a wide range of organisational and personal issues, Resource Manager enables those responsible for running a Learning Centre to achieve 'expert' status from the first contact with users and potential users.

Is Resource Manager currently in use?
Launched in late 1996 after many months of trial and improvement, Resource Manager is being used and implemented by several major national, public and private sector organisations. Details can be supplied.

What does it run on?
Resource Manager is designed to run on Microsoft Access; a popular, versatile and effective platform.

Can it be tailored for my organisation?
Yes, no two designs for Resource Manager are the same. Options and alterations to screens, fields, terminologies, data, product analysis, equipment number & type and user analysis reports are available.

LEARNING RESOURCES INTERNATIONAL LTD

For further information or to arrange a trial demonstration, please contact:

UK Head Office
Bamfords Yard, Turvey, Bedford MK43 8DS
Tel: (01234) 888877 Fax: (01234) 888878

London Office
Duncan House, High Street, Stratford, London E15 2JB
Tel: (0181) 215 0707/8 Fax: (0181) 215 0709

Resource Manager has been developed in conjunction with Harwood Consultancy Ltd.

Index

activity-based resources 66–8
administration 83–134
administrator
  best person for the job 91
  credibility factor 91–2
  recruiting 91
  role of 92
  training 91
alternative media 66–8
alternatives 8
audio 42

bonus-related system 28
books 101
  protection 47
  relating to training
    programmes 47
  resistance to reading 48
  selecting 46
  versus alternative options
    45–9

breakfast launch 126–7
budgets 20–21, 52, 101

career development 64
case studies 135–67
  Heathrow Airport Limited
    159–64
  London Ambulance
    Service (LAS) 142–8
  Royal Marsden NHS Trust
    135–41
  Sims Education Services
    Ltd 165–7
  Victoria and Albert
    Museum 154–8
  Virgin Atlantic Airways
    149–53
catalogues 73–4, 87–9
  entry formats 187–8
CBT 45, 58
CD-I 45, 54–6, 68, 76, 101,

120
benefits 55
future of 56
CD-ROM 39, 45, 51–3, 63,
    68, 76, 89, 101, 109, 110,
    117, 119, 120, 129
evaluating 57
celebrities at launch 79
change
    accepting 8
    continual process of 17
    in culture 10
    preparing the way for 9–10
    staged approach 15–17
classroom-based training 4
colour coding systems 74
communication 68
Compact Disk Interactive
    (CD-I) 54
competitions 30–31, 76–8,
    129
corporate video 31–2
cost analysis 21
cost of setting up 20–21
costs 51–9, 54
    Internet 65–6
Credit Suisse 98
customer service inventory 31
cybercafé, 65–6

damaged goods 29
database 111
demand versus supply 93–6
departmental days 123
development champions
    11–12

development support tables
    28
discounts 102

e-mail 116
evaluation form 84
evaluation process 83–6, 95
    manager's role 86
events, marketing 108–9

failure, reaons for 14
family access 115–16
feedback
    from users 35
    launch 81
feedback sheets 83–5, 85–6
financial support 21
freebies 14–15, 78

games 66–8
    team-building 68

health and safety materials
    68–9
Heathrow Airport Limited,
    case study 159–64
hire 116
Honey, Peter 70, 109
hours of opening 27–8

induction process 117–18
information age 53
information technology (IT)
    59, 111
    awareness 34
    systems 87

insurance policy 29
international open learning
    centres 107
Internet 64–5, 116
    costs 65–6

job for life 4
journals 69–70

language learning 118–19
language resources 62–3
launch 75–82
    agenda 80
    breakfast 126–7
    celebrities at 79
    checklist 80, 82
    feedback 81
    formal presentations 80
    invitations to attend 77–8
    key principles 77
    multiple sites 106
    objective 76
    planning 77
    posters 202–3
    prelaunch, questionnaire
        174–5
    programme ideas 82
    repetition 82, 109–11
    see also relaunch
LEAP 102
learning advisers 103–4
learning bus 123
learning centre
    checklist for need 9
    future 133–4
    networks 92

reason for setting up 5,
    33–5
recommended materials
    179–80
learning club 127–30
learning environment 97–100
learning incentives 130–32
Learning log 70
learning material evaluation
    form 170–73
learning networks 132–3
Learning Resources
    International 20
learning skills, books on 179
learning styles 70, 180–81
    preferences for 30
logistics 73–4, 83–134
London Ambulance Service
    (LAS), case study 142–8

mailshots 111
management exercises 67
management of the learning
    centre 90–91
management systems 87
market research 8, 27
marketing 15, 29–32
    events 108–9
    multiple sites 106–7
materials, *see* resources
measurement methods 85
media selection 34–5
meetings 116
mini-learning centre 123
mobile unit 123
monitoring process 95

motivation 4, 132
multimedia 51–9
  advantages of 53
multiple centres, resource
  selection 105
multiple sites 104–7
  launch 106
  marketing 106–7
  promotion 105
multi-skilling 34
music 100

needs analysis 8, 34
needs identification 7–12
new products, promotion 126
newsletters 31, 124–5
non-vocational materials
  61–72
number of copies to purchase
  95

obstructions 10
open learning centre 2–3, 7
opening hours 27–8
opposition 10

periodicals 69–70
permitted development time
  27
posters 102
  launch 202–3
prelaunch, questionnaire
  174–5
professional qualifications 69
project leader 24
promotion

multiple sites 105
new products 126
roadshows 120–23
promotional materials 78–80,
  102

questionnaires 29–30, 122
  prelaunch 174–5
  service 89–90

reference/library system 34
relaunch 82, 109–11
reports on usage 85–6
resistance, dealing with 10–12
resource-based learning 1–4,
  95
resource evaluation 35
Resource Manager 87
  sample screens 191–200
resources
  assessing suitability 36–7
  evaluating 37
  relevance to job 36–7
  selecting 105
  types available 41–9
  utilisation 39–40
resources fair 38–9
resourcing the learning centre
  33–40
retirement, targeting 113
revision facilities 119–20
revolving libraries 56–7, 94
roadshows, promotion 120–23
Royal Marsden NHS Trust,
  case study 135–41

Scope 101, 102
security 28
self-development 3–5, 7, 62,
    76, 131, 132
  fair 110
  transition to 15
  trial 15
  workshops 11–12
self-diagnostics 59
self-motivation 62
self-worth 4
selling the idea 13–17
senior managers
  commitment from 27
  involvement 17, 32
  resources for 70–72
  support from 13–15
service questionnaires 89–90
Sims Education Services Ltd,
    case study 165–7
size of learning centre 25–6
social events 127–30
software selection 53–4
space limitation 100–102
starting the project 23–32
study skills 70
  books on 179
subject areas to cover 96
support 13–15, 102–4

targeting
  retirement 113
  women 111–13
  younger employees 113–14
Tarragon 57
team-building games 68

technology 53
technology awareness
    workshop 71
technology-based training 52
technology change 52
technology days 116–17
time element 39
timescales for setting up
    19–20
training courses 4
  complementing 97
Training Direct 57, 102
trial-sized package 14–15

usage evaluation 85–6
usage prediction 95–6
usage reports 85–6

Victoria and Albert Museum,
    case study 154–8
video
  assessment 43–5
  environment effect 44–5
  evaluating 45
  for potential users 31–2
  humour versus drama 43–4
Virgin Atlantic Airways, case
    study 149–53
vouchers 28

WIIFM (what's in it for me?)
    factor 28
Win Win 68
women, targeting 111–13
workbooks 41–2, 68
working parties 23–5

checklist 25
delegating responsibilities
    25
mixed group 24

Xebec 57

younger employees, targeting
    113–14

Zeneca 110

A **Unique** Total Strategy Approach
for Learning Resource Centres...

*...from the UK's leading Independent advisor and supplier of
Resource Based Learning and Self Development Strategies.*

Learning Resources International are
uniquely placed to provide objective advice
based on comprehensive knowledge, and
access to the widest available range of
international products. Combining extensive
staff experience in Training and Development
and Self Development fields and a background
in marketing, logistics and OLC/LRC cultures,
Learning Resources International provide
an essential independent service to anyone
considering issues around Resource Based
Learning and Self Development.

*Learning Resources International offer a
consultancy partnership to provide advice, ideas
and solutions in the following key areas of
Resource Based Learning:*

- Project co-ordination and management
- Product and resource indices and manuals
- Competency or CSF/KSF matching
- Product selection and acquisition
- Organisational logistics, I.T. management
  and 'Expert' Systems
- Training design and delivery for Learning
  Support staff
- Marketing initiatives
- Materials update service
- Evaluation and assessment mechanisms
- Development Plan integration
- Internal and external support and advice

LRI
LEARNING RESOURCES INTERNATIONAL LTD
"Helping You to Help Others"

For more information contact
Learning Resources International Ltd. at:

*U.K. Head Office
Bamfords Yard, Turvey, Bedford MK43 8DS
Tel (01234) 888877 Fax (01234) 888878*

*London Office
Duncan House, High Street, Stratford, London E15 2JB
Tel (0181) 215 0707/8 Fax (0181) 215 0709*

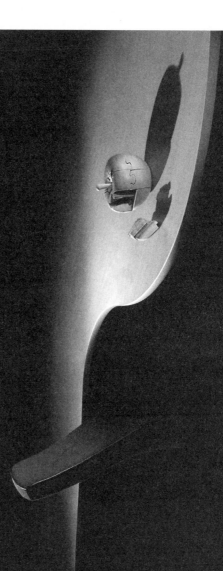